AUTHORS

Paolo Crippa (23 April 1978) has cultivated his passion for Italian history since high school. His research interests are focused mainly in the field of military history and in particular on italian armored units from the 30s until the end of World War II. In 2006 he published his first volume, "I Reparti Corazzati della Repubblica Sociale Italiana 1943/1945", the first organic research carried out and published in Italy on the subject. In 2007 he published "Duecento Volti della R.S.I." and in 2011 " Un anno con il 27° Reggimento Artiglieria Legnano". He regularly contributes to several journals: Milites, New Historica, SGM - World War II, Batailes & Blindes, Armoured Vehicles and history of the twentieth century, Mezzi Corazzati, both as an author, or in collaboration with other researchers. He published with the editor Mattioli 1885 in 2014 "Italy 43 – 45 – Civil War improvised AFV's" (2014), "Italian AFV's of the Civil War 1943 - 1945" (2015) and "Italy 43 – 45 – AFV's and MV's of co-belligerent units" (2018).

Carlo Cucut was born in Nole (TO) in 1955. He cultivated a passion for history as a boy and over the years has deepened this interest by dedicating himself to historical research. He published articles in the italian magazines: "Storia del XX Secolo", "Storie & Battaglie", "Milites" and "Ritterkreuz". He published various volumes for Marvia Edizioni: "Penne Nere on the eastern border. History of the Alpini's Regiment "Tagliamento" 1943-1945 ", winner of the "De Cia" Award; "Attilio Viziano. Memories of a war correspondent "; "Armed Forces of RSI on the eastern front"; "Armed Forces of RSI on the Western Front"; "Armed Forces of RSI on the Gothic Line"; "Alpini in the City of Rijeka 1944-1945". For the Trentino Modeling Group he published "The armed forces of RSI 1943-1945. Land forces ".

PUBLISHING'S NOTES

None of unpublished images or text of our book may be reproduced in any format without the expressed written permission of Luca Cristini Editore (already Soldiershop.com) when not indicate as marked with license creative commons 3.0 or 4.0. Luca Cristini Editore has made every reasonable effort to locate, contact and acknowledge rights holders and to correctly apply terms and conditions to Content.
Every effort has been made to trace the copyright of all the photographs. If there are unintentional omissions, please contact the publisher in writing at: info@soldiershop.com, who will correct all subsequent editions.
Our trademark: Luca Cristini Editore©, and the names of our series & brand: Soldiershop, Witness to war, Museum book, Bookmoon, Soldiers&Weapons, Battlefield, War in colour, Historical Biographies, Darwin's view, Fabula, Altrastoria, Italia Storica Ebook, Witness To History, Soldiers, Weapons & Uniforms, Storia etc. are herein © by Luca Cristini Editore.

LICENSES COMMONS

This book may utilize part of material marked with license creative commons 3.0 or 4.0 (CC BY 4.0), (CC BY-ND 4.0), (CC BY-SA 4.0) or (CC0 1.0). We give appropriate attribution credit and indicate if change were made in the acknowledgments field. Our WTW books series utilize only fonts licensed under the SIL Open Font License or other free use license.

For a complete list of Soldiershop titles please contact Luca Cristini Editore on our website: www.soldiershop.com or www.cristinieditore.com. E-mail: info@soldiershop.com

Title: **THE BALTIC FOGGING BATTALIONS 1942 - 1945**
Code.: **WTW-049 EN** By Paolo Crippa and Carlo Cucut
ISBN code: 9791255890232 first edition: October 2023
Language: English, size: 177,8x254mm Cover & Art Design: Luca S. Cristini

WITNESS TO WAR (SOLDIERSHOP) is a trademark of Luca Cristini Editore, via Orio, 35/4 - 24050 Zanica (BG) ITALY.

WITNESS TO WAR

THE BALTIC FOGGING BATTALIONS 1942 - 1945

PHOTOS & IMAGES FROM WORLD WARTIME ARCHIVES

PAOLO CRIPPA - CARLO CUCUT

BOOKS TO COLLECT

CONTENTS

Fogging as a defence weapon 5

The Fogging Battalions of the Royal Army in Germany 7

The military research centre in Peenemünde 11

Reaction to the Armistice 23

Fogging units during the R.S.I. 25

History of the units 45

    Fogging Troop Command 45

    Fogging Troop Training Centre (Ausbildungstager) 45

    I Fogging Battalion 46

    II Fogging Battalion 49

    III Fogging Battalion 51

    IV Fogging Battalion 52

    V Fogging Battalion 53

    Women's Auxiliary Service Unit 53

    Organigram according to Giorgio Pisanò 54

Casualties 67

Fogging Divisions' uniforms 69

The Chemical Service of the R.S.I 70

Testimonials 71

Documents 87

Bibliography 97

FOGGING AS A DEFENCE WEAPON

The appearance of the air weapon on the battlefields required the major states to urgently find countermeasures to deal effectively with the new threat.

During the First World War, the air force was essentially employed for air supremacy and observation tasks, while bombing actions, due to the small payload carried by aircraft or airships, as well as the poor accuracy of rudimentary targeting instruments, were relegated to demonstrative actions or those with a modest war effort.

It was in the Second World War, however, that, thanks to the considerable advances in aircraft and targeting instruments, aerial bombardment became fundamental in the various theatres of operation, both in the tactical and strategic fields.

Ports, airports, viaducts, railways and railway marshalling yards, factories and infrastructure in general, as well as population centres of course, became the main targets of air raids.

The defence against the threat posed by bombing aircraft was, and still is, essentially of two types:

- active - with aircraft sent to intercept enemy bombers and anti-aircraft guns arranged to defend the target(s)
- passive - with appropriate means to camouflage and/or conceal the target(s), protect personnel and the population

The aforementioned defences were the responsibility of the Air Force and Anti-Aircraft Artillery, for the active part, and the Corps of Engineers for the passive part.

On 1 July 1923, the Royal Army set up the Military Chemical Service within the Corps of Engineers and, from 1934, a Chemical Company and a Flame Throwing Platoon were included in each Army Corps. In the same year, a Chemical Department was also established, which was transformed into a Chemical Regiment in 1936 and remained operational until September 1943.

The Chemical Regiment, stationed in Rome, had the task of training and training battalions in both gas warfare and the use of chemicals used in battle, developing equipment and means suitable for their use.

Among the specialist battalions formed and trained by the Chemical Regiment were the fog battalions. The task of the units belonging to the fog battalions was to obscure the target from the view of enemy aircraft crews, sent to carry out bombing actions, by forming an artificial fog.

Artificial fog is the product of a chemical composition derived from the combined use of smoke-producing substances. By smoke-producing (or fogging) we mean certain substances that have the property of condensing the moisture in the air, forming a true artificial fog. It is a highly corrosive liquid consisting of a mixture of sulphuric anhydride and sulphuric chlorohydrin. The sulphuric anhydride, dissolved in sulphuric chlorohydrin, is emitted into the atmosphere where, by condensing the moisture, it forms a fog consisting of tiny droplets of sulphuric acid. The fog thus produced, strongly acidic due to the presence of hydrochloric acid and sulphuric acid, is highly irritating, especially near the source of emission.

In order to achieve effective obscuration, however, it was necessary to consider numerous variables: the size of the area to be obscured, the morphology of the terrain, wind, humidity, temperature, the topoaerological environment, the seasons, and the direction of the air attack. All these variables had to be evaluated during the planning stage for the deployment of the fog units and the equipment to be used, with the aim of maximising the result at the site to be protected.

The Fog Units were initially deployed in the immediate vicinity of sensitive targets, later extending their deployment in depth, even kilometres, around the area to be protected, due to the increased intensity and precision of the air offensive.

There were basically three types of equipment used to produce artificial fog:
- fog equipment for ground positions
- fog equipment installed on vessels as mobile sources
- special-purpose electric-pump fog equipment

All the equipment included: compressed air cylinders as pressure tanks, pressure reducers to ensure the flow of air into the containers, transfer apparatus for filling the fog liquid containers and the compressed air cylinders, and protective clothing to be used during duty.

THE FOGGING BATTALIONS OF THE ROYAL ARMY IN GERMANY

It is little known to the public that, in 1942, the German General Staff requested the dispatch to the German Baltic Sea coast of two Fogging Chemical Battalions of the Royal Army Corps of Engineers to protect the industrial plants stationed there. This was the only occasion on which the Germans explicitly requested the support of specialists from the Italian Armed Forces, as they recognised their efficiency and superiority over similar German units.

Between October and December of that year, accepting the OKW's request, the S.M.E. decided to send two Fogging Battalions to Germany and thus the 2nd Battalion and the 3rd Battalion were transferred:

- II Fog Battalion - deployment: Gotenhafen[1], in the Gulf of Gdansk in the Baltic Sea, with detachments in Memel[2] and Pillau - Commander: Major Calafiore
- 3rd Mist Battalion - deployment: in Wilhemshaven, North Sea, with detachments in Emden - commander: Major Madau

Each Battalion consisted of three or four Operations Companies and a Command Company, for a strength of about a thousand men per Battalion, with a total strength of about 2,000 men, specialised in the use of fog machines.

Battalion II used equipment and equipment brought from Italy, while Battalion III used Italian equipment and German equipment. The main German equipment for the production of artificial fog, used by the Italian sappers, were: N.P.G. 42, N.T.D. 32, N.P.G. 42 type equipment with an electric pump for ground operation, equipment installed on board vessels. Individual armament was the standard equipment of the Italian soldier of the time: rifle or musket mod. '91, pistol Beretta mod. 34 and machine gun Breda 30.

The Battalions, which operated alongside the Flak and Kriegsmarine and came from the Rome Chemical Regiment, depended tactically on the Naval Commander of their respective strongholds, a Kriegsmarine admiral, and the task of the Foghorns was the passive defence of their sector, concealing ports and vital industrial and military installations (including factories and ramps of the deadly V-1 and V-2) with artificial fog curtains, thus protecting them from the threat of enemy air raids. Each Battalion Company was entrusted with a sector of several square kilometres; each sector was set up with appropriate artificial fog lines and an extensive radio and telephone communication network was set up, which allowed contact not only between the positions, but also with the Company and Battalion Command, which was responsible for sending the orders for action. Numerous passive defence plans were devised, which took into account the different directions in which the wind could blow and the various targets that needed to be hidden from enemy aircraft.

---
1 Gotenhafen is the current Polish city of Gdynia.
2 Memel is the current Lithuanian city of Klaipéda, the main port of Lithuania.

Since there was also significant sea traffic, both warships and Uboats, a number of dummy targets were also prepared to attract enemy aviation.

Starting in February 1943, the German armed forces set up a liaison office at the Mogens Command with the task of coordinating activities.

▲ Letter sent to Italy by a soldier serving in the 3rd Fogging Battalion on 14 December 1942: very interesting the stamps of the Battalion Command (web source).

▼ Franchise postcard sent to his family by a soldier of the 41st Company, then in the 3rd Fogging Battalion, on 8 March 1943. Interesting the stamp of the 41st Fogging Company, with the words "Office without stamp" (private collection).

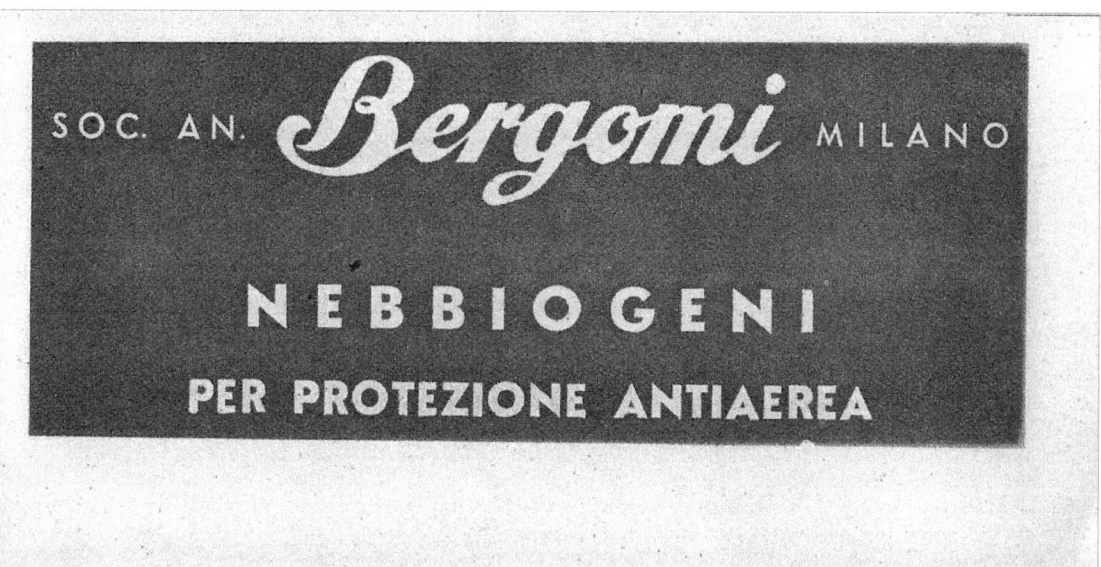

▲ It is curious to note how the fog gas for concealment was also advertised by the manufacturers (in this case the Società Anonima Bergomi of Milan) in the press intended for 'civilians': this advertisement, in fact, appeared in an issue of the magazine 'Sapere' in 1937.

▼ 15 May 1943 (private collection).

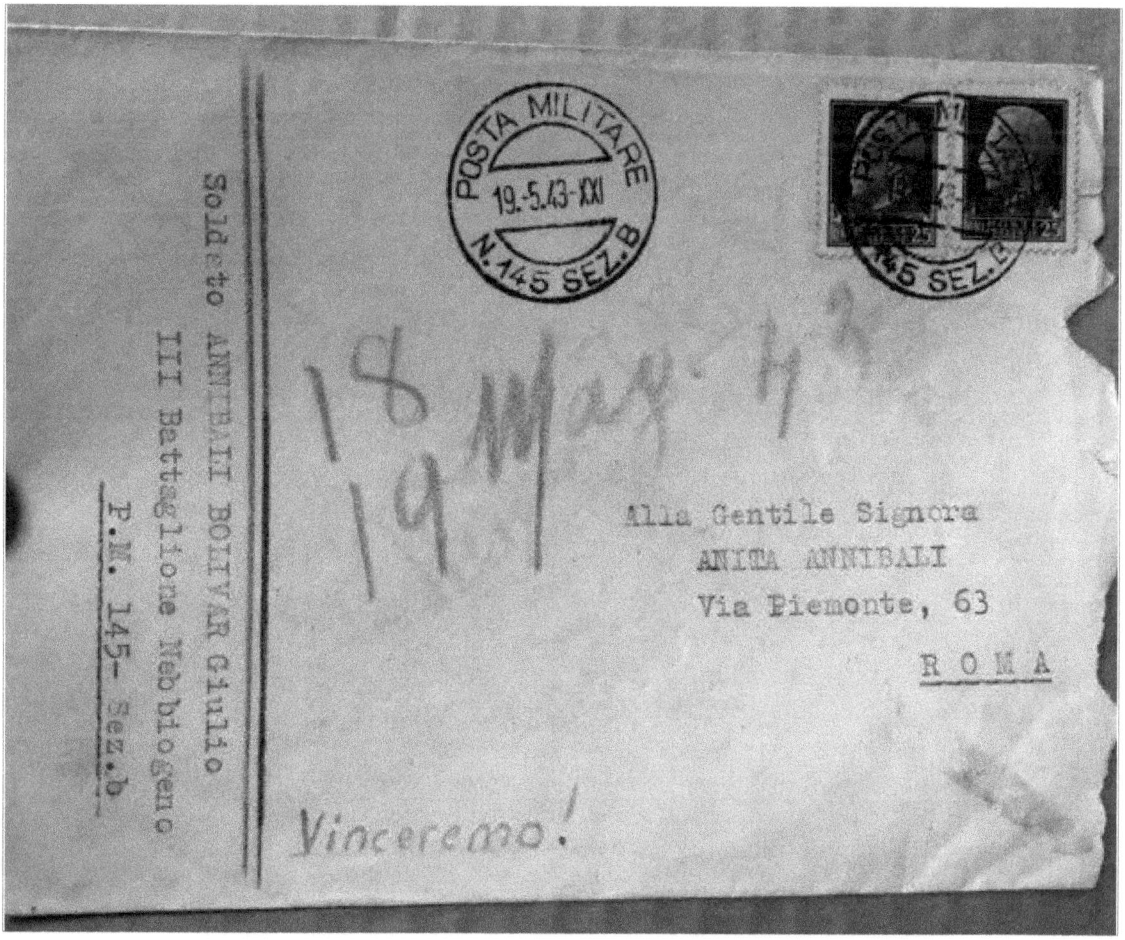

▲ Stamps of the 3rd Fogging Battalion on a postcard, sent from Germany on 23 July 1943. The Military Post stamp bears the number 145 - section B, typical of the Foggings, while, less visible is the linear stamp of the 39th Company of the 3rd Battalion, which bears the double indication in Italian and German "3° BATTAGLIONE NEBB. - 3. NEBELBATTAILON" and "39th Company Nebb. - 39. Nebelkompanie" (private collection).

▼ Aerial photograph of a bombing target covered by artificial fog. One can see the effectiveness of the fog covering the target from the view of the bombing planes' pointers.

THE MILITARY RESEARCH CENTRE IN PEENEMÜNDE

During the Second World War, Peenemünde was home to the Heeresversuchsanstalt, a large missile testing and development site established in 1937. Previously, the research team, led by Wernher von Braun and Walter Dornberger, had operated in Kummersdorf, south of Berlin. However, the Berlin base had proved too small for experiments. So a new site was sought to host the research and Peenemünde was chosen. The new one, located on the coast, allowed rockets to be launched and subsequently monitored across more than 300 kilometres of open water. Here, until the end of the war, German scientists developed the basis of rocket technology and two deadly weapons, the first missiles, the famous V-1 and V-2 flying bombs: the first was developed by the Luftwaffe in Peenemünde-West, the second by the Heer. Test launches of the first V-1 missile took place in early 1942 and the first V-2 (then called A-4) was first launched on 3 October 1942, from Prüfstand VII. Many other technologies were developed at the Peenemünde site, perhaps the most important of which was closed-circuit television, which was used on the V-2 launch pads to follow the rocket launches. On the island, where more than 15,000 people worked (1943 figure), there was one of the largest liquid oxygen production plants, its own coal-fired power station, which supplied the power for the entire missile centre, the largest wind tunnel in Europe, missile launch sites, rocket control and monitoring facilities (in the north-east area) and numerous bunkers.

To protect the site, as we have seen, two battalions of the Regio Esercito specialised in the use of fog bombers were sent in October 1942, with the task of concealing the site from Allied bombers.

The base remained secret for a long time, until its presence was revealed, in a manner not entirely clear: officially all information was gathered thanks to British air reconnaissance[3]. However, from then on, the site became a target for Allied air raids.

The heaviest occurred on the night of 17-18 August 1943 (Operation Hydra), when more than 500 RAF heavy bombers struck the installations in three waves, dropping almost 2,000 tons of bombs, 85% of which were highly explosive munitions. The bombing cost the lives of 732 unarmed civilians working at the site, including Walter Thiel, head of rocket engine development and a number of German specialists. Most of the bombs were in fact mistakenly dropped on the settlement and fields of foreign workers, forced labour forced by the Germans to work at the site[4]. The air fleet involved in the raid would have consisted of 596 bombers

---

3 Testimonies and documents claim that the existence of Peenemünde was discovered thanks to the work of Polish clandestine army intelligence (Armia Krajowa or AK) and information from other sources (including a Danish pilot who allegedly photographed something resembling a V rocket), but British intelligence denied for years after the war that it had received any information about Peenemünde from Poland. Copies of the AK reports did, however, emerge in Poland after the war (the originals were kept in Britain) and from some of them it was deduced that many of the Polish workers in the fields around the rocket site were none other than Allied informants belonging to the AK. In recent times, the British authorities have stated that all AK reports have been destroyed and therefore it is impossible to ascertain the truth.
4 213 prisoners died: 91 Poles, 23 Ukrainians, 17 French and 82 concentration camp prisoners of unidentified nationality.

(324 Lancaster, 218 Halifax and 54 Stirling), of which 94 were 'Pathfinders'. At the same time as the attack on the V-1 and V-2 bases, 8 De Havilland DH.98 Mosquitoes conducted an attack on Berlin, with the aim of diverting most of the German fighters away from the main target, succeeding in keeping them away for the first two waves and, indeed, the German night fighters were diverted confusingly to Bremen, Wilhelmshaven, Kiel, Berlin, Rostock, Swinemünde and Szczecin. During the operation, the British lost 47 aircraft, most of them during the third wave, when the German night fighters had finally moved into the vicinity of the area, after the Luftwaffe had realised what the main target of the attack was. Despite this, Bomber Command had not started the attack in the best possible way: the Pathfinders aimed incorrectly about three kilometres south of the dormitories, which were nevertheless hit by the bombs, causing, as we have seen, hundreds of casualties; the production facilities suffered marginal damage while the design workshops and administrative offices suffered more than 50 per cent damage.

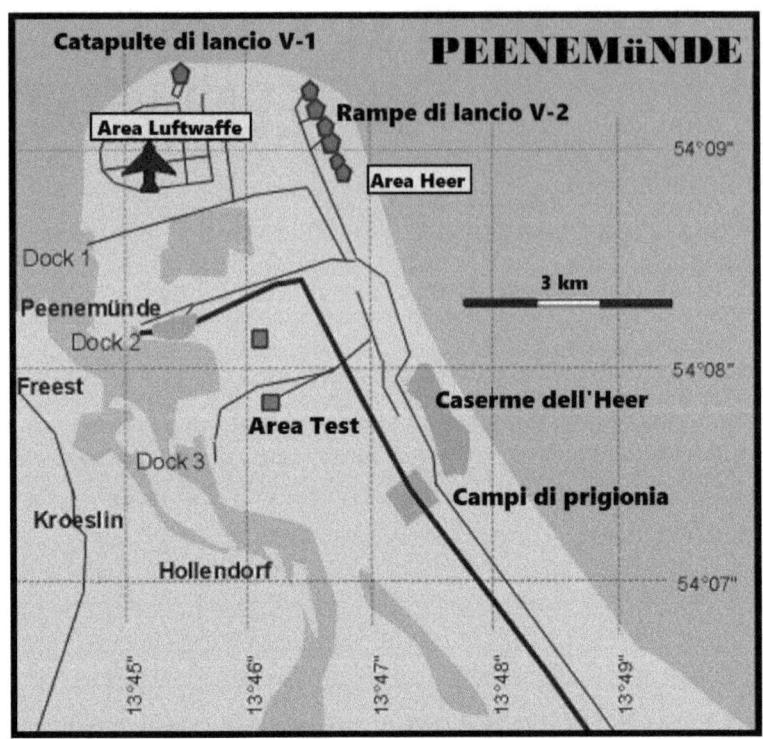

▲ This diagram gives an idea of the layout of the elements that formed the research centre on the island of Usedom.

The USAAF proposed to General Arthur Harris, commander of the Royal Air Force's Bomber Command, to carry out a second raid on Penemünde on 19 August, but the British general refused, as he was convinced that he had achieved a brilliant success.

Due to the serious error of judgement and the damage suffered by the Peenemünde facilities, Luftwaffe Deputy Commander, Colonel General Hans Yeshonnek, responsible for the organisation of the air defence system in the region, took his own life 19 August.

The tremendous raid prompted the Germans to move the production of V rockets underground, into the Hartz Mountains. Despite the frequent raids, many installations in Peenemünde remained largely intact until the end of the conflict; the last V-2 rocket was launched from Prüfstand VII in Peenemünde 14 February 1945.

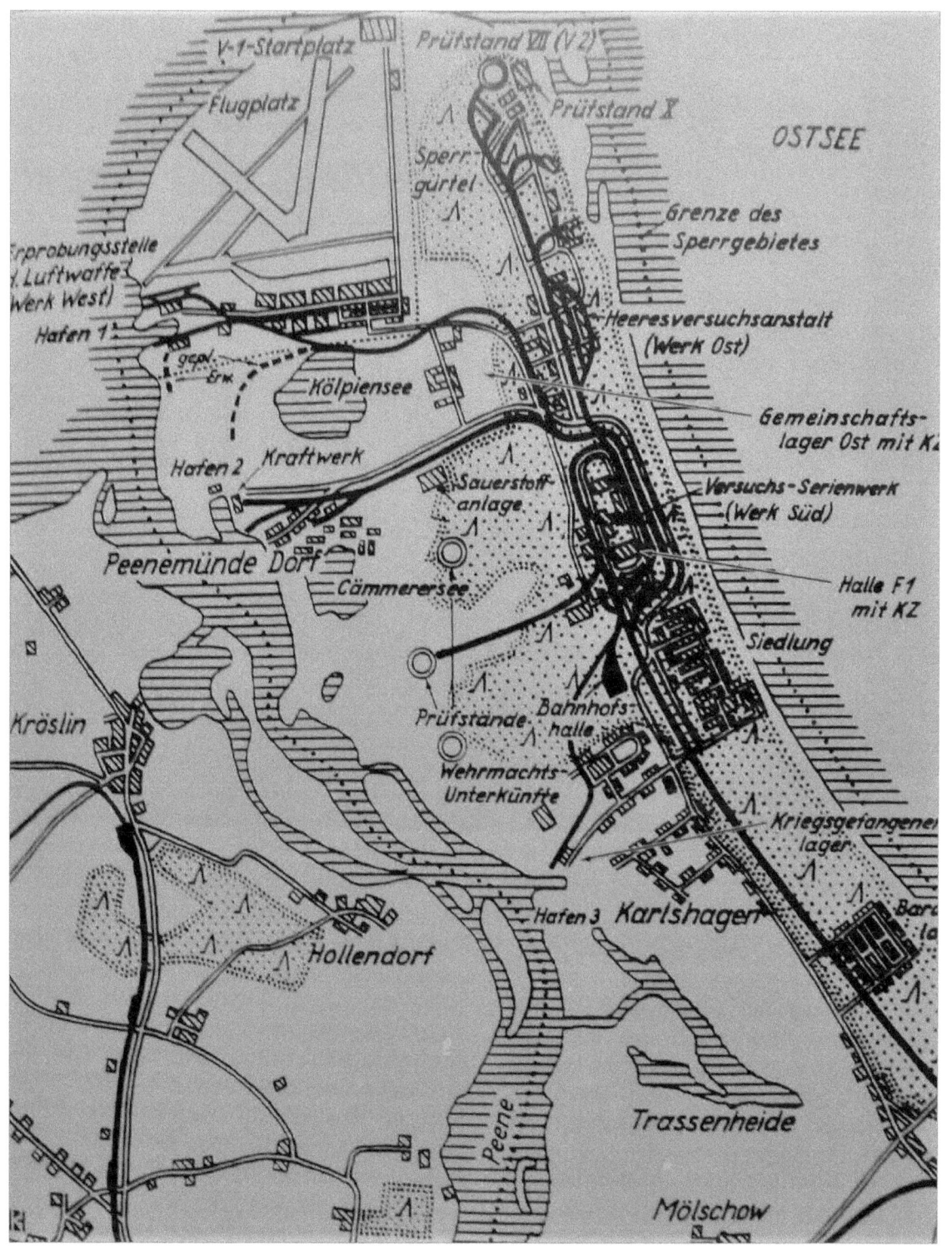

▲ Map detailing the Raketenzentrums in Peenemünde in 1943: the vastness of the area and the articulation of structures and buildings is striking.

▲ Photograph taken on 12 June 1943 by the R.A.F. aerial reconnaissance of Prüfstand VII (test launch area) in Peenemünde.

▼ Interior of a factory in Peenemünde, some V-2 cylinder heads under construction can be seen.

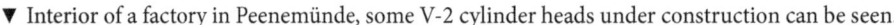

▲ A V-1 missile in flight: the V-1 study was conducted by the Luftwaffe.

▼ In August 1945, the Peenemünde site was badly damaged and apparently abandoned.

▲ Launch of a V-2 rocket from the Peenemünde base.

▲ Photograph taken by the British air reconnaissance of the Peenemünde area in April 1943 in preparation for the bombing of 'Operation Hydra' (Web source).

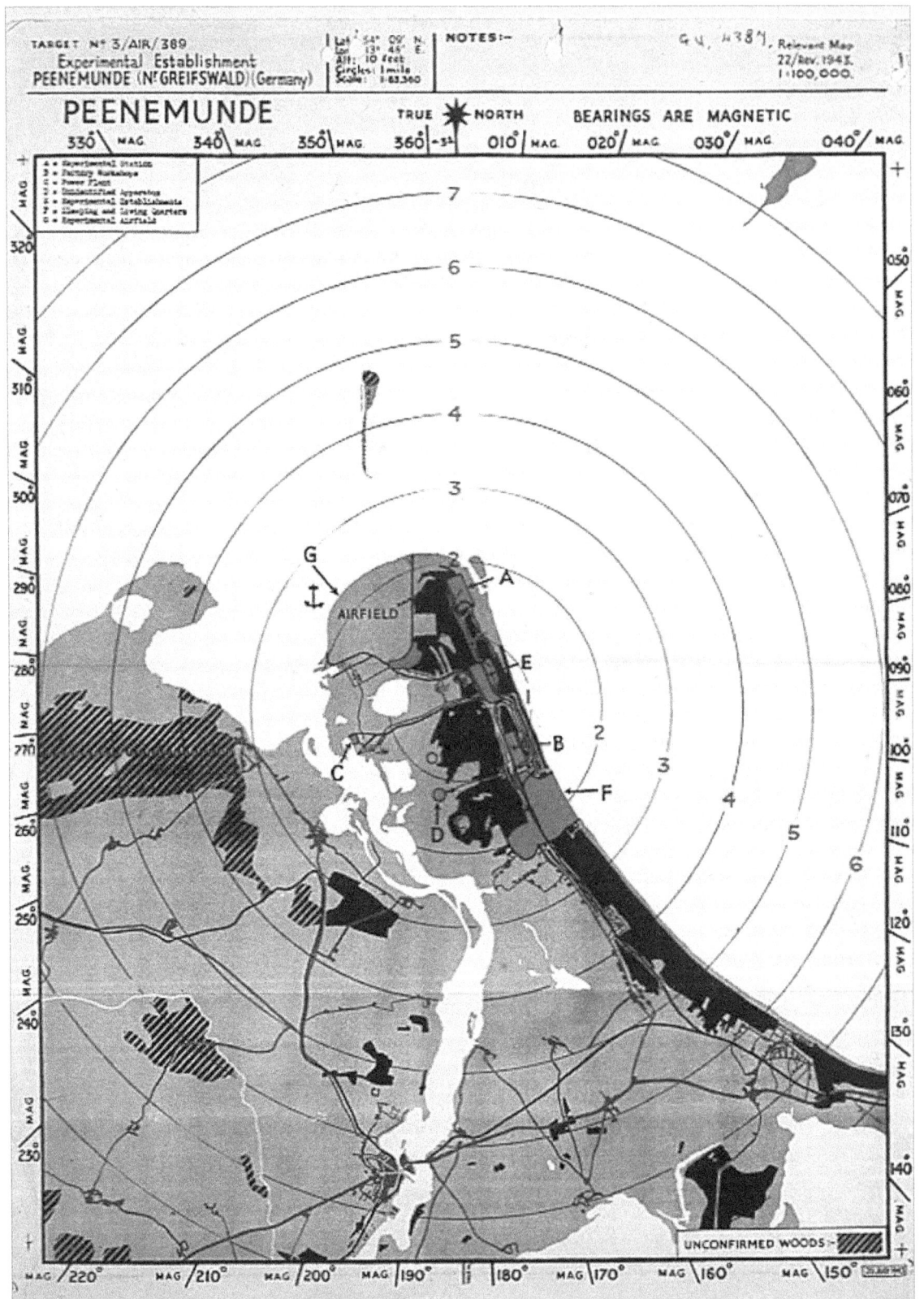

▲ Map of the Operation Hydra bombing area on the night of 17-18 August 1943 (Web source).

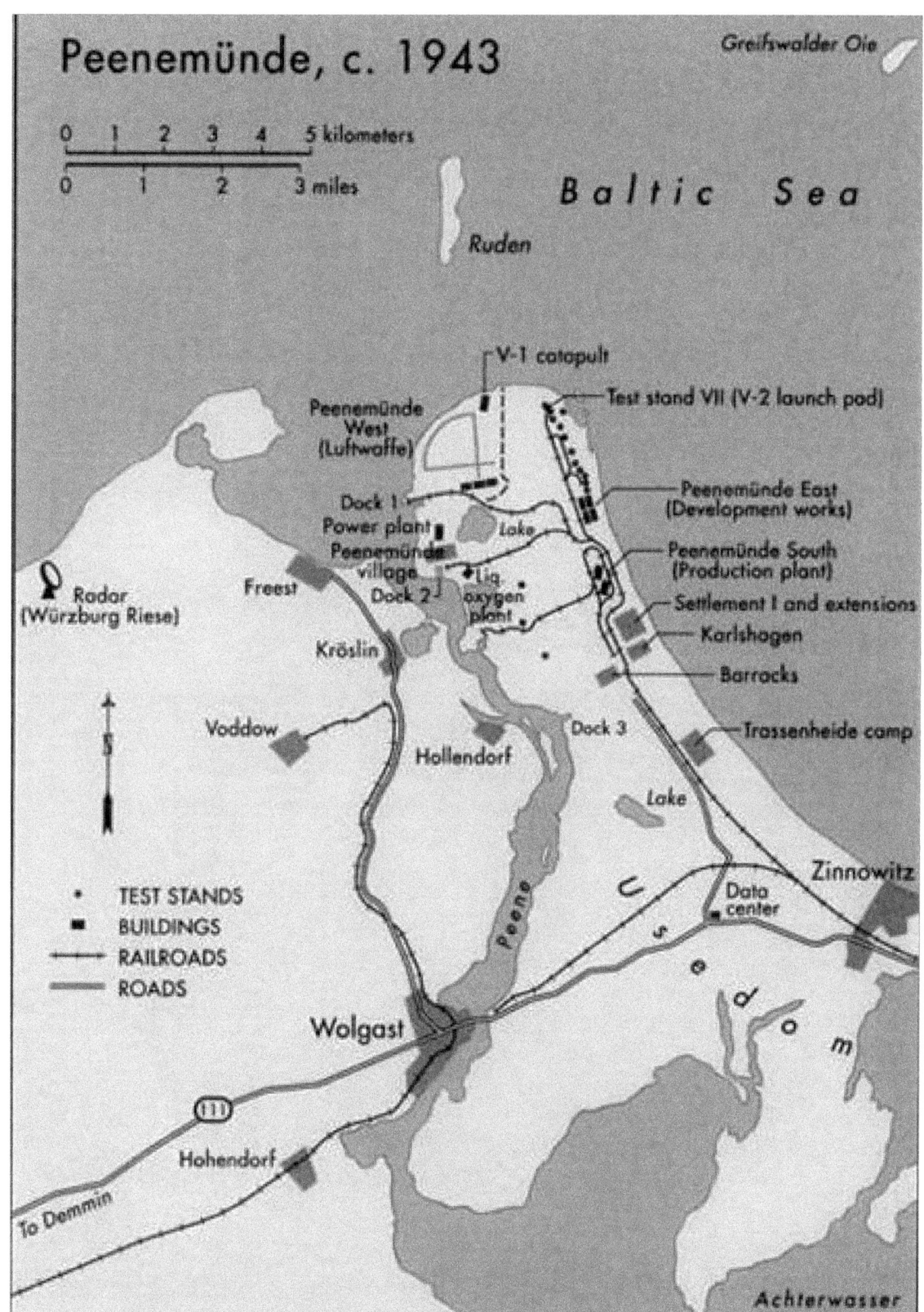

▲ Map of the Peenemünde area with the roads and railway sections that allowed the transport of material and workers involved in the construction of the V-1 and V-2 (Web source).

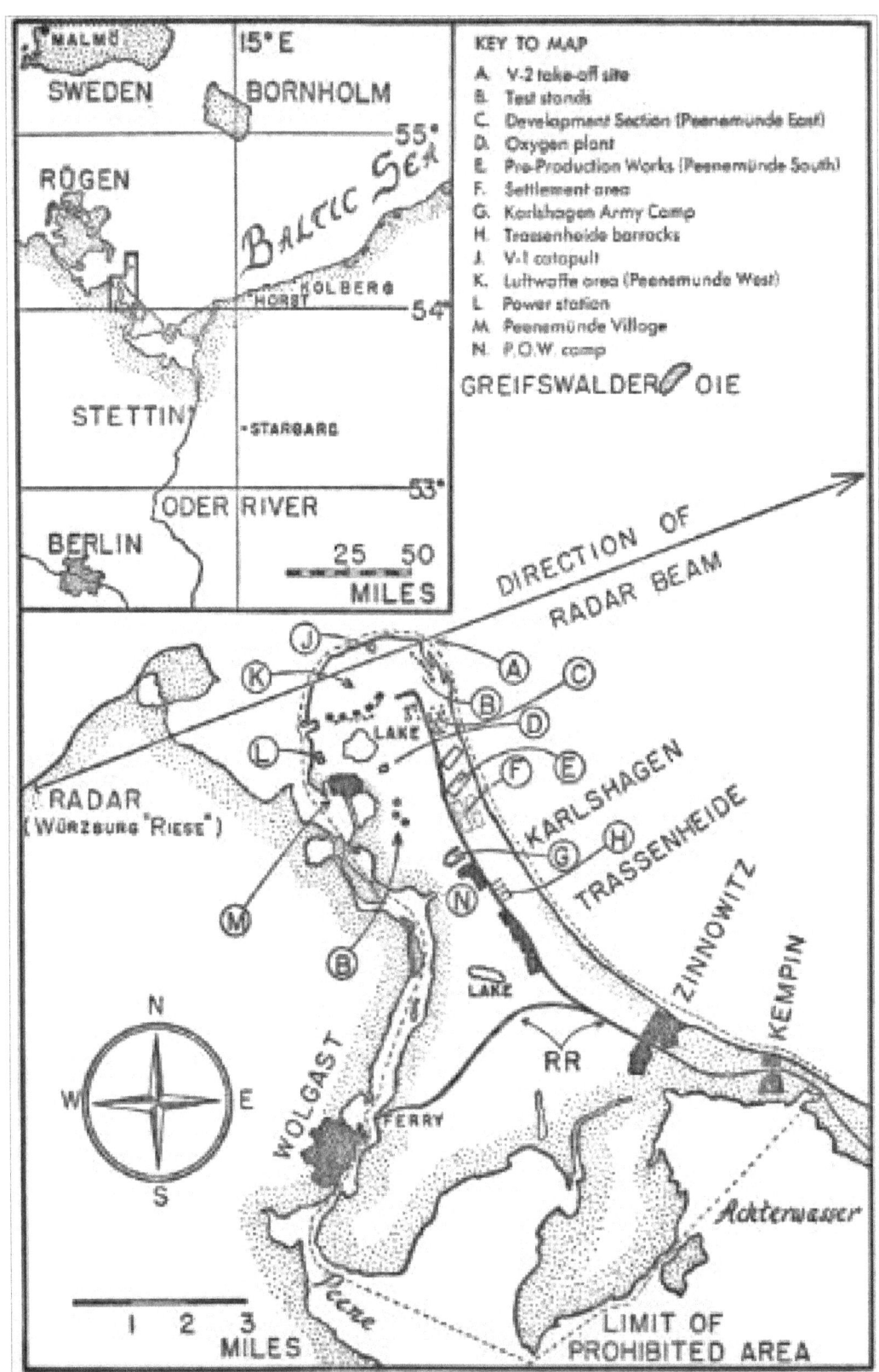

▲ English map showing the limit of the area to be bombed and the direction of the bombardment.

▲ During the night between 17 and 18 August 1943, the Peenemünde complex suffered heavy bombing by the Royal Air Force, which only partially damaged the missile facilities. This aerial photo shows Peenemünde, taken by an R.A.F. scout a few days before the bombing.

▼ A photograph of Peenemünde, after the Bomber Command raid. The picture, taken from a De Havilland Mosquito PR Mark IX of RAF 540 Squadron, using an F.52 type vertical camera (36"), shows the frightening concentration of bomb craters on the airport and the damage inflicted on the Luftwaffe's technical buildings at Peenemünde West.

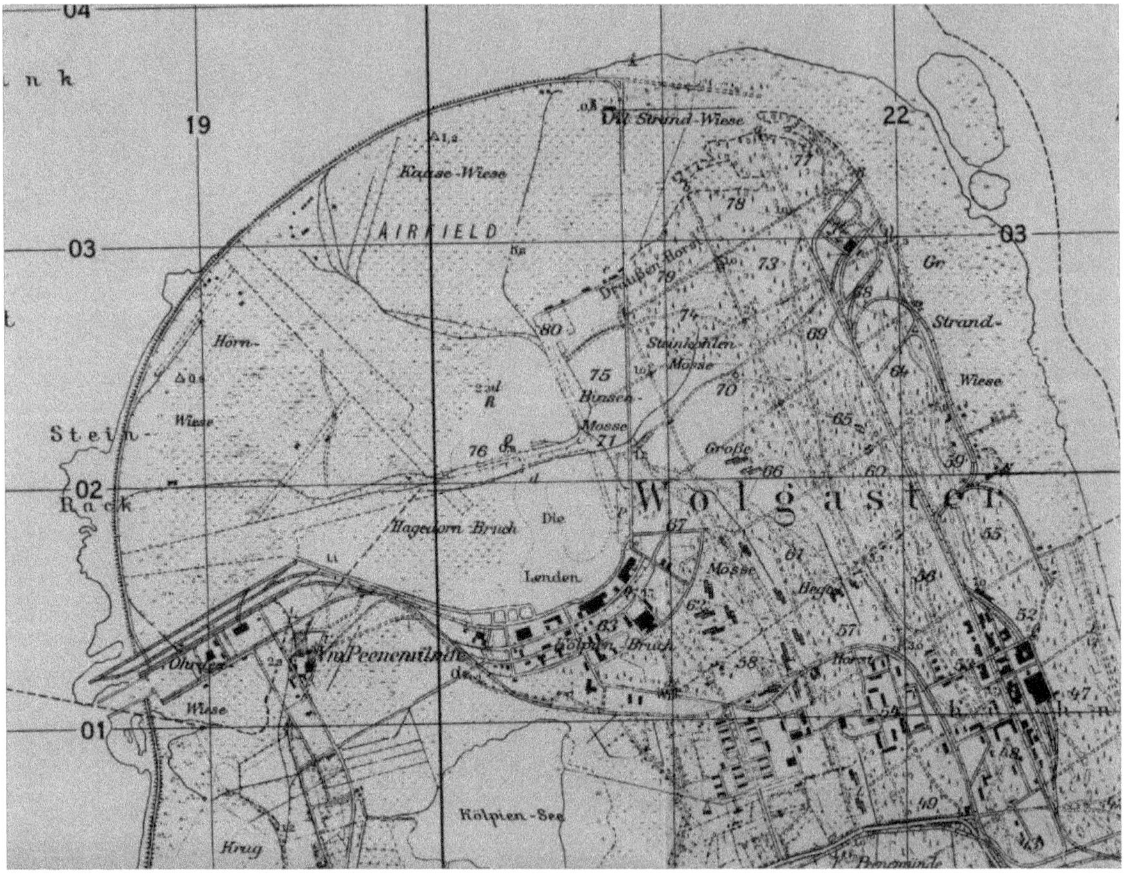

▲ The Peenemünde research area in a map from a 1952 US correspondence.

▼ The Peenemünde Missile Centre today converted into a Science and Technology Museum.

REACTION TO THE ARMISTICE

On the night of 8 September, after hearing Badoglio's proclamation on the radio and only being reached by the echo of what was really happening in Italy, the Battalion commanders gathered the officers, asking them to consult the non-commissioned officers and dependent soldiers, to determine what to do at that difficult juncture. The next morning, it became clear that the almost unanimous decision was to continue fighting with the German Armed Forces, but keeping the Italian uniform and flag. Thus, a communiqué was sent to the German Square Command, informing them of the decision to continue the conflict, but with a number of conditions:

- Until the existence of an Italian higher command was established, from which orders could be taken, the two Fog Battalions were to be considered autonomous from the Germans and, therefore, absolutely independent.
- As a result, the Battalions would not recognise any disciplinary provisions from any Germanic Command and would continue to respect and apply the Italian Army Discipline Regulations, under the sole responsibility of the Major, commander of the Battalions.
- Officers, non-commissioned officers and troops would have kept the standard Italian uniform, without the slightest variation, with their weapons.
- At Battalion Headquarters, the Italian flag would be raised regularly and no restrictions of any kind would be placed on the functioning of the Command and relations with the German Commands.

The conditions demanded by the Fogging Battalions were accepted without reservation by the Commander of the stronghold: preserving unaltered uniforms and flags, the Italian units thus continued their war, alongside the German Armed Forces, in the most absolute independence and without any solution of continuity between the period before the Armistice and the one immediately following, remaining autonomous and without any connection with superior Italian Commands. It should also be noted that, while the 3rd Mist Battalion, stationed in Wilhelmshafen, and the Danzig Submarine Command immediately sided with Germany, in the 2nd Battalion, anti-German propaganda began to spread, so the commander, Major Calafiore, decided to expel the pro-Badoglian elements (5 officers and 19 non-commissioned officers and troops), having them interned by the Germans, to avert the risk of a change of front. Commander Calafiore, in the following months, carried out an intense propaganda activity for enrolment in the Fogging among Italian soldiers, who were in the Italian Military Interned (I.M.I.[5]) camps in the region, also distributing his own 5-page typescript, entitled 'Notiziario per i militari italiani internati' (Newsletter for Italian military internees).

---

[5] I.M.I.: Italian Military internees, were the soldiers captured by the Germans after 8 September 1943 and deported to concentration camps. Captured Italians never obtained the status of prisoners of war, but were always considered as internees.

It should be noted that, after the armistice of 8 September 1943, the commander of the BETASOM Naval Base in Bordeaux, by virtue of an agreement with Admiral Karl Dönitz, formed the 1st Atlantic Riflemen Division of the National Republican Navy and obtained the assignment of 6.000 Italian Military internees to the Kriegsmarine to set up Bau Battalions on the Atlantic coast and another 5,400 to reinforce the Fogging Battalions in the Baltic, as well as the liberation of 4,000 interned sailors (I.M.I.) in the Trier and Neubrandenburg camps, who had asked to join the Social Republic. In fact, numerous members of the Neubrandenburg divisions formed after the Armistice came precisely from the prison camps: the writer Giovanni Guareschi, in his diary of imprisonment, entitled '*The Great Diary*', recounts the episode of a large group of Genieri, detained by the Germans as IMIs, who joined the Social Republic en masse, came out of the reticulated camp where they were imprisoned, framed in marching step and singing 'Giovinezza' to rejoin the Fogging divisions in the Baltic.

The 39th Company of the 3rd Battalion was reached by the news of the formation of the Italian Social Republic through the radio and some of its members, knowing the characteristics of the new flag, worked to make a tricolour loaded with the black eagle with the republican fasces with claws, which was probably the first banner of the newly formed fascist state to fly outside the national territory.

The activity of the two Fogging Battalions continued uninterrupted even during this phase in which the units remained de facto autonomous from any higher command and was even much more intense, because the air attacks on the German base at Wilhemshaven became increasingly frequent and violent. The fog engineers operated so efficiently, however, that the Allied war bulletins often had to record the impossibility of verifying the effectiveness of some bombing missions on their intended targets, precisely because of the thick blankets of artificial fog that covered the German bases in the Baltic and North Sea during the raids. During these months, the Fog Battalions suffered numerous losses, mainly due to the fact that the soldiers found themselves operating daily during the air raids practically in the open, until the artificial fog blankets covered the areas targeted by the attacks.

FOGGING UNITS DURING THE R.S.I.

The situation changed radically in February 1944, when a Training Camp (Ausbildungslager) for Fogging Troops was set up in Szczecin and the relative Fogging Troop Command, initially held ad interim by Major Giuseppe Calafiore of the 2nd Battalion, later replaced by Colonel I.G.S. Carlo Fedi. Major Calafiore had been in Germany since October 1942, as commander of the 2nd Fogging Battalion, stationed at Gotenhafen-Gdynia in the Gulf of Gdansk, but, while awaiting the arrival from Italy of the designated Commander Colonel Fedi, he directed the headquarters of the Fogging Troops Command for several months. The two Fogging Battalions thus lost their complete autonomy, becoming dependent on this Command; for the German Armed Forces, the Fogging took on the name 'Italienische Nebeltruppen in Baltikkustenland'.

At the Fogging Troop Command, the German armed forces established a liaison office, consisting of a major, a second lieutenant and two troop soldiers, who knew Italian. This O.K.M. Liaison Office, set up by the M.M.I. and commanded by Colonel Trillini, had a twofold task: to check directly on the spot that the employment and treatment of Italian soldiers complied with the agreements between the O.K.W. and the R.S.I., to inform the Command of problems that arose at the battalions so that it could intervene to remedy them.

The training camp organised by the engineers was considered so valuable that it also trained Kriegsmarine personnel; the most valuable instructor of the Ausbildungslager was Major Calafiore. In January 1944, Major Calafiore had also drafted an operational manual for the Baltic Foghorns, in the form of a secret memoir entitled *'Memoir for the training of Italian cadres and units employed in the German War Navy'*. It is a guide, based on the doctrines of the 1940s, to the organisation of the fogging of military targets, to be distributed not only to Italian military personnel, but also to Kriegsmarine officers, during the training course.

The Italian Military Mission in Germany operated under the command of Colonel (later General) Chief of Staff Umberto Morera. The Mission was made up of officers, non-commissioned officers and soldiers of various arms, with its Operational Headquarters in Berlin, where it had been established in 1944, and six Liaison Units at the OKW, OKL, OKM, OB/Ost, OB/Süd-Ost and OB/West. It worked to protect interned Italian soldiers, to turn them into free workers or to facilitate their repatriation (in cooperation with the Red Cross), to track down Italian soldiers who, individually or in small groups, were in the German Armed Forces, to repatriate them or transfer them to departments of the Social Republic and, finally, to coordinate and supervise the training of the four Italian Divisions in Germany and of the units operating abroad, such as the Mist Battalions. The Mission's activities were conducted amidst serious difficulties, both because of the objective situation of hardship (Germany was subjected to heavy and continuous bombing, aggravated by the looming Red Army over Berlin from January 1945) and because of the blatant attitude of contempt and mistrust with which Italian soldiers were treated by the German authorities. The Italian Military Mission was present and active in Berlin until 10 April 1945, when it left the city due to the beginning of the Soviet encirclement.

The oath of allegiance to the R.S.I. took place, in almost all places on 9 February 1944, the anniversary of the first Roman Republic, but the 2nd Battalion, the reason for which is unknown, did not take the oath until 22 June, more than four months after the date set for the official swearing-in of the Armed Forces of the Social Republic.

In March 1944, a new Battalion was formed, Battalion I, commanded by Captain Raffaele Di Pietro and with Lieutenant Giosuè Cuccurullo as adjutant, which was sent to the naval base on the island of Usedom - Wollin[6] . This Battalion was formed from specialists already in Germany and from recruits from German military internment camps, reaching a strength of more than 400 sappers. The I Battalion, which was praised by the German Command for its tenacious behaviour, protected both the Baltic submarine base and the V-1 and V-2 launching ramps, located at the northern end of the island Usedom in Karlshagen, at the famous Peenemünde base.

On 23 June 1944, the day after the swearing-in of the 2nd Battalion, a report was sent to Marshal Graziani's Secretariat, in which the situation of the Fogging units deployed in Germany was indicated. From this report, it can be seen that the wards and personnel were as follows[7] :

- Fogging Troop Command and Liaison Unit with the OKM - Szczecin
- II Battalion - Szczecin: 130 officers, 49 non-commissioned officers, 184 graduates/soldiers
- on the North Sea in Wilhelmshaven: 29 officers, 34 non-commissioned officers, 368 graduates/soldiers
- on the Baltic Sea in Swinemünde[8] : 26 officers, 23 non-commissioned officers, 340 graduates/soldiers
- on the Baltic Sea at Gotenhafen: 32 officers, 30 non-commissioned officers, 338 graduates and troops
- at Heydebrekk: 32 officers, 79 non-commissioned officers, 701 graduates/soldiers
- in Zeit (near Leipzig): 6 officers, 17 non-commissioned officers, 228 graduates/soldiers

a total of: 255 officers, 232 non-commissioned officers, 2159 graduates/soldiers - 2,646 military personnel[9]

In July 1944, the Fogging departments received an inspection visit from the Italian Military Mission in Germany, led by Lieutenant Commander Alfredo Saidelli; in his report of 24 July, the officer reported not only on their location and training situation, but also pointed out that the presence of Italian, French and Slavic military internees in a detention camp, located not far from the Fogging Troop Training Centre, was negatively affecting the morale of the Republican soldiers.

---

6 Wollin is the present-day Polish island of Wolin, which divides the Szczecin Lagoon from the Baltic Sea, together with the neighbouring island of Usedom, an island in the Baltic Sea on the German-Polish border.
7 In the report written for Marshal Graziani's Secretariat, the number of the deployed Battalion, apart from the II, is never mentioned. Not even the post-war rapporteur of the report gave an answer as to why this was missing.
8 Swinemünde is the present-day town of Świnoujście, a Polish enclave on the German island of Usedom.
9 The high number of officers present stems from the high percentage of prisoner officers, in the camps near Szczecin, who opted to join the Italian Social Republic.

A report of 25 October 1944, written by Captain Umberto Bruzzese after his visit to the Fogging Battalions, again on behalf of the Italian Military Mission in Germany, pointed out, among other observations, that the units had a large surplus of officers, many of whom had expressed the wish to return to Italy, and that Major Calafiore was disliked by many officers and troop soldiers, without specifying the reason.

By Decree No. 868 of 27 October 1944, the War Tribunal was established at the 2nd Mist Battalion, headed by Major Giuseppe Calafiore; the Military Attaché in Berlin, however, became the addressee of any appeals and consequently had the power to suspend the execution of sentences and, for officers, to order the transfer of the trial to Italy.

At a later date, two more Battalions were formed, the 4th and 5th, bringing the total number of Battalion personnel to over 2,000. The latter two units were stationed in inland areas of Germany, the 4th at Fedderwardergroden and the 5th at Zeit, near Leipzig, to protect vital petrochemical plants, which produced special synthetic petrol for aviation use. The 5th Battalion was instrumental in defending these installations from a devastating British air attack, described by one witness as '*a veritable ocean of* fire'[10] on the night of 16-17 January 1945.

A group of Auxiliaries also arrived from Italy, of whom unfortunately no information is available, and complements from the Chemical Troops Depot in Verona, who made it possible to replace both the fallen and the soldiers repatriated from Germany due to illness or physical unfitness, which occurred during operational activity, which entailed considerable risks, not only due to the danger caused by the enemy, but also due to the use of dangerous chemicals[11].

The task performed by the Fogging Battalions was characterised by high technicality and great risk, requiring a high degree of training. Wrapped in protective anti-acid combinations, the Foggings were able to lay down a thick chemical curtain of chlorhydrin in just 50 seconds. The units were stationed on a very extensive operational front, which had been meticulously designed and equipped with small shelters, consisting of barracks and disused railway wagons, which, in addition to serving as makeshift accommodation, contained and protected all the special equipment necessary for artificial fogging, so that it was always ready for use, in the positions predetermined by the passive defence plans.

There was little or no contact with Italy, so much so that many of these soldiers were long considered to be fallen or missing by their families.

In the first months of 1945, the situation in Germany began to deteriorate abruptly, as the great Anglo-American offensive from the West and the Soviet offensive from the East developed ever more violently, while the territory controlled by the German Armed Forces shrank more and more. In particular, the beginning of the year saw the Red Army begin the final offensive that took it to Berlin: Hungary was conquered and, within a single month, Poland. On 3 February Soviet troops reached the Oder, preparing for further offensives that led to the conquest of Vienna on 13 April, Berlin on 2 May and Prague on 9 May.

---

10 See '*Fogging Battalions of the R.S.I. up to 3 May 1945 in Northern Europe*' by Remo Zara in ACTA No. 21 (May/July 1993), Historical Institute of the RSI.
11 Information taken from circular letters from the EMS and the Undersecretariat of State for the Army on soldiers belonging to fog units, repatriated from Germany due to illness and physical unfitness in February 1945.

In the prospectus of the Italian Military Mission's report of January/February 1945, the location and staffing of the fog divisions are reported:
- Fogging Troop Command and Liaison Unit - deployment: Wilhelmshaven - personnel: 5 officers, 3 NCOs, 9 graduates/soldiers
- SAF Auxiliary Unit
- Training Centre - location: Wilhelmshaven - personnel: 48 officers, 38 non-commissioned officers, 171 graduates/soldiers
    - Command Company
    - 51st Company
- I Battalion - deployment: Swinemünde - personnel: 19 officers, 29 non-commissioned officers, 418 graduates/soldiers:
    - Command Platoon
    - 34th Company
    - 35th Company
- II Battalion - deployment: Gotenhafen - personnel: 30 officers, 67 non-commissioned officers, 629 graduates/soldiers:
    - Command Platoon
    - 29th Company
    - 32nd Company
    - 33rd Company
    - 41st Company
- III Battalion - deployment: Wilhelmshaven - personnel: 22 officers, 39 non-commissioned officers, 477 graduates/soldiers:
    - Command Platoon
    - 38th Company
    - 39th Company
- IV Battalion: Command Platoon, 28th Company
- Wilhelmshaven - 10 officers, 26 non-commissioned officers, 225 graduates/soldiers
- 40th Company - deployment: Swinemünde - personnel: 5 officers, 23 non-commissioned officers, 204 graduates/soldiers
- 37th Autonomous Company - deployment: Emden - personnel: 8 officers, 16 non-commissioned officers, 217 graduates/soldiers
- 52nd Autonomous Company - deployment: Zeit - personnel: 5 officers, 20 non-commissioned officers, 177 graduates/soldiers

A total of: 154 officers, 261 non-commissioned officers, 2527 graduates/soldiers - 2,942 military personnel.

▲ The 2nd Fogging Battalion was only able to swear in Szczecin on 22 June 1944, four months later than all other units of the R.S.I. In the centre of the picture, Major Giuseppe Calafiore, commander of the unit (Arena Archive).

▼ Colonel Carlo Fedi, commander of the Fogging Battalions, during a visit to his units, probably in April 1945. The senior officer held the rank of general and, according to some sources, was promoted to the higher rank before the end of the conflict. The officer in the background should be Major Calafiore commander of the 2nd Fogging Battalion (Arena Archive).

▲ Two Foggings pose wearing clothing, essential in carrying out fogging activities, to protect the human body from the effects of chemical agents: rubber overalls and gloves, and a gas mask, here contained in a special bag to be worn over the shoulder (Pisanò Archive).

▼ Some soldiers of the Fogging Battalions were instructed in the use of the Panzerfaust by German naval officers: in the last weeks of the war, the Italian engineers were forced to fight even as simple infantry units (Pisanò Archive).

▲ A group of young girls from the Women's Auxiliary Service, probably serving in the 3rd Fogging Battalion (Pisanò Archive).

▼ The same Auxiliaries as in the previous picture, portrayed without their grey-green cloth jackets, in front of the barracks that served as accommodation for the unit (Pisanò Archive).

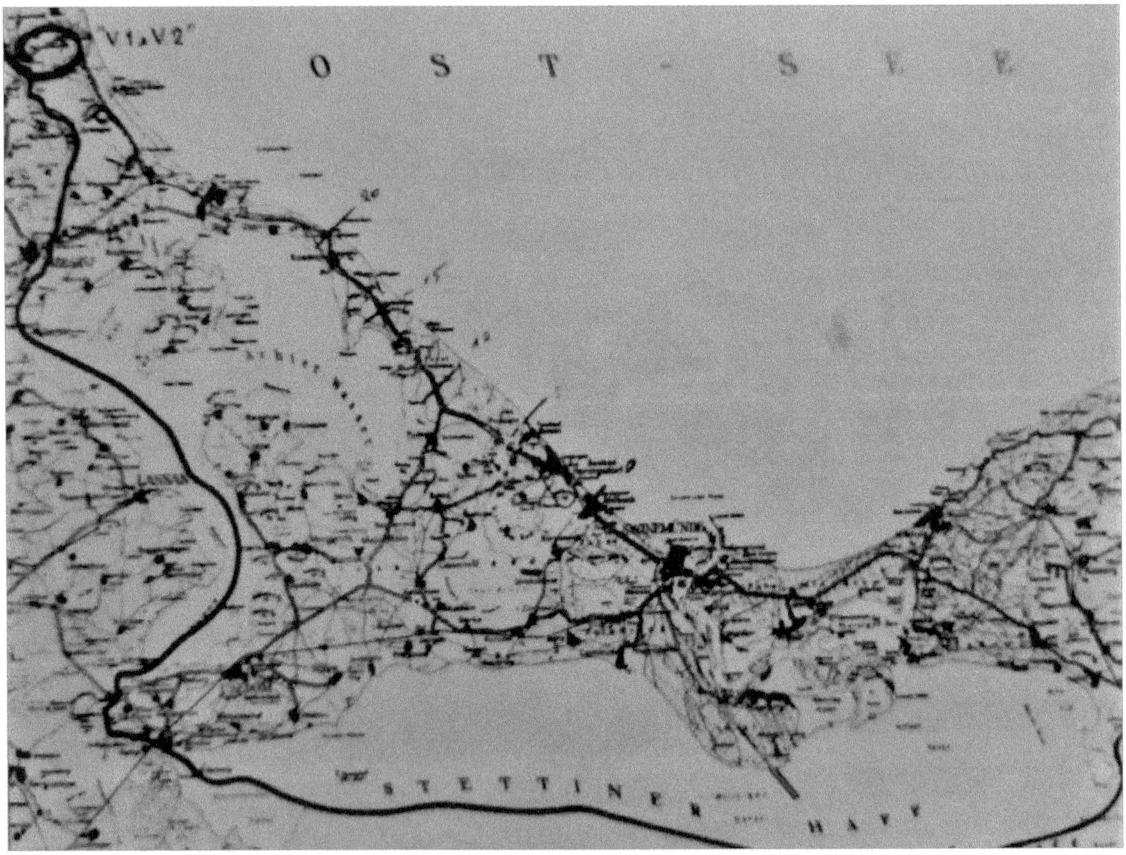

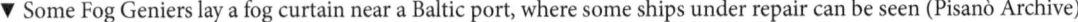
▲ German wartime map showing the layout of the facilities at the Peenemünde site (Pisanò Archive).

▼ Some Fog Geniers lay a fog curtain near a Baltic port, where some ships under repair can be seen (Pisanò Archive).

▲ A closer image highlights the equipment used to create the artificial fog (Arena Archive).

▼ The group of Foggings, portrayed in the previous pictures, return to their quarters at the end of the operation (Pisanò Archive).

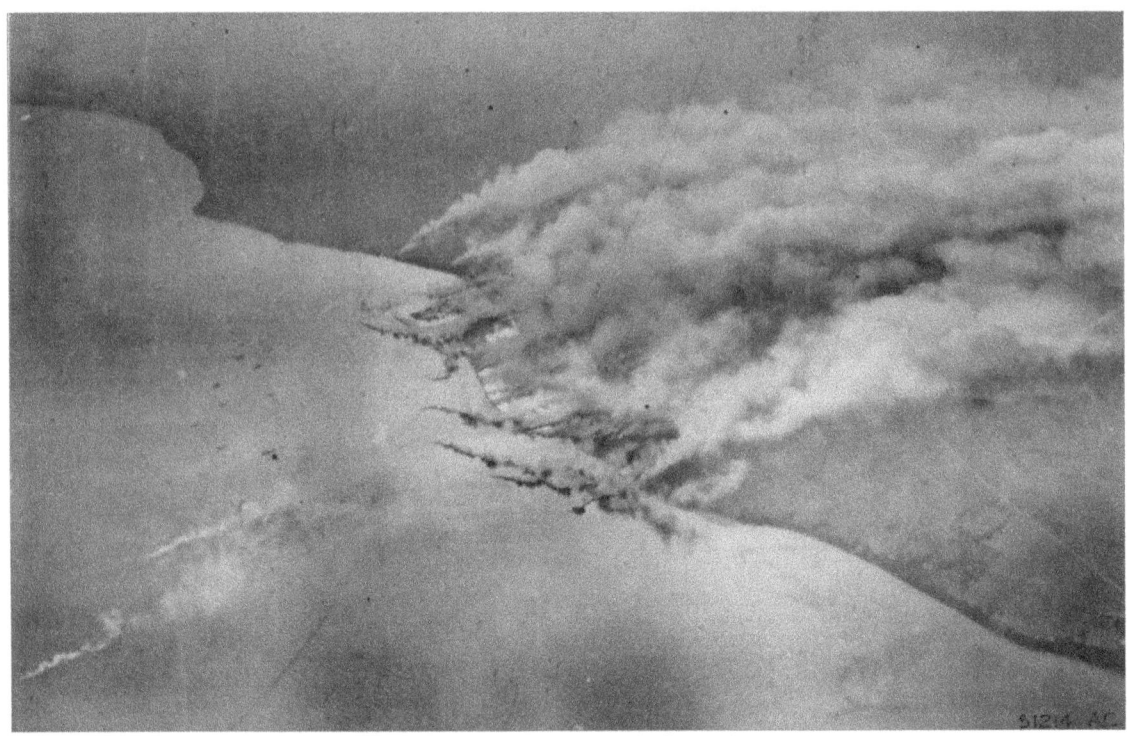

▲ Fog installations belonging to the 2nd Battalion in action at Gotenhafen (web source).

▼ The 3rd Fogging Battalion in action at Wilhelmshaven during a bombing raid by American B-17s (web source).

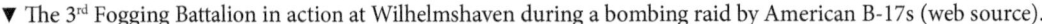

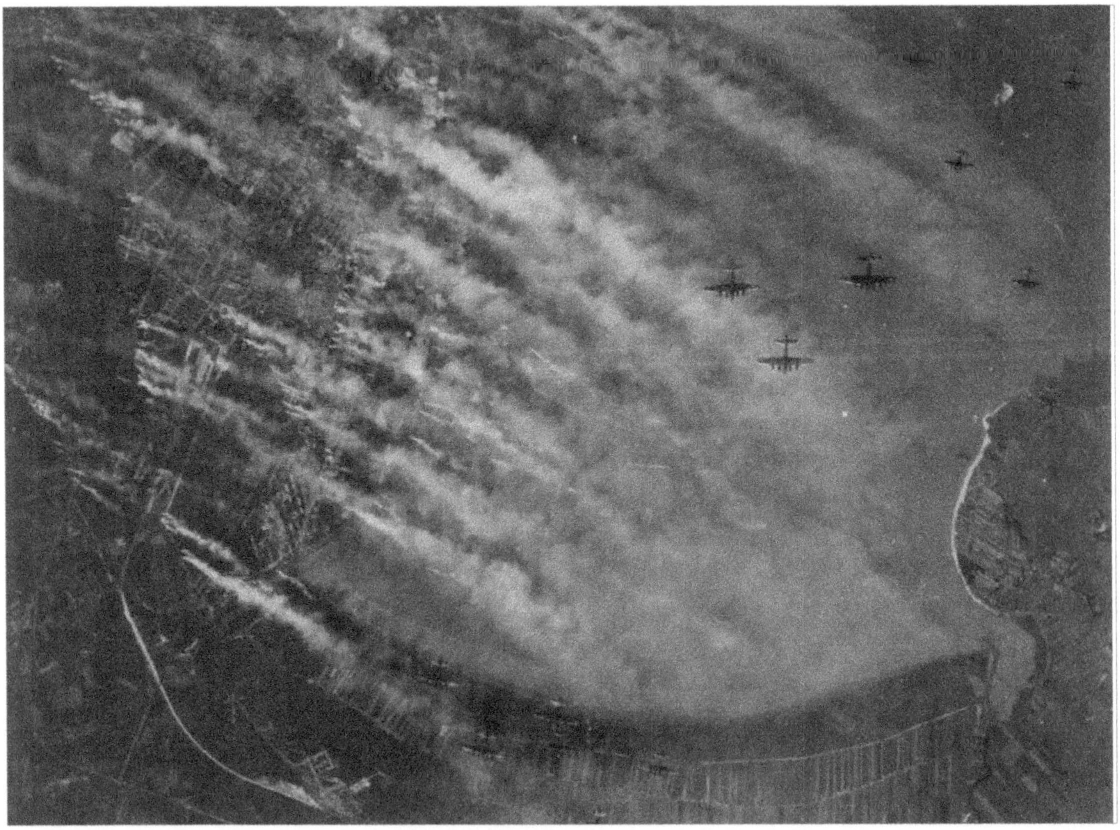

▲ Letter sent to Italy by a soldier serving in the 3rd Fogging Battalion in 1944: the unit can be identified by Feldpost number 81226.

▼ Letter sent by a soldier belonging to the 2nd Fogging Battalion stationed in Gotenhafen in 1944 or 1945, given the destination Alpenvorland (web source).

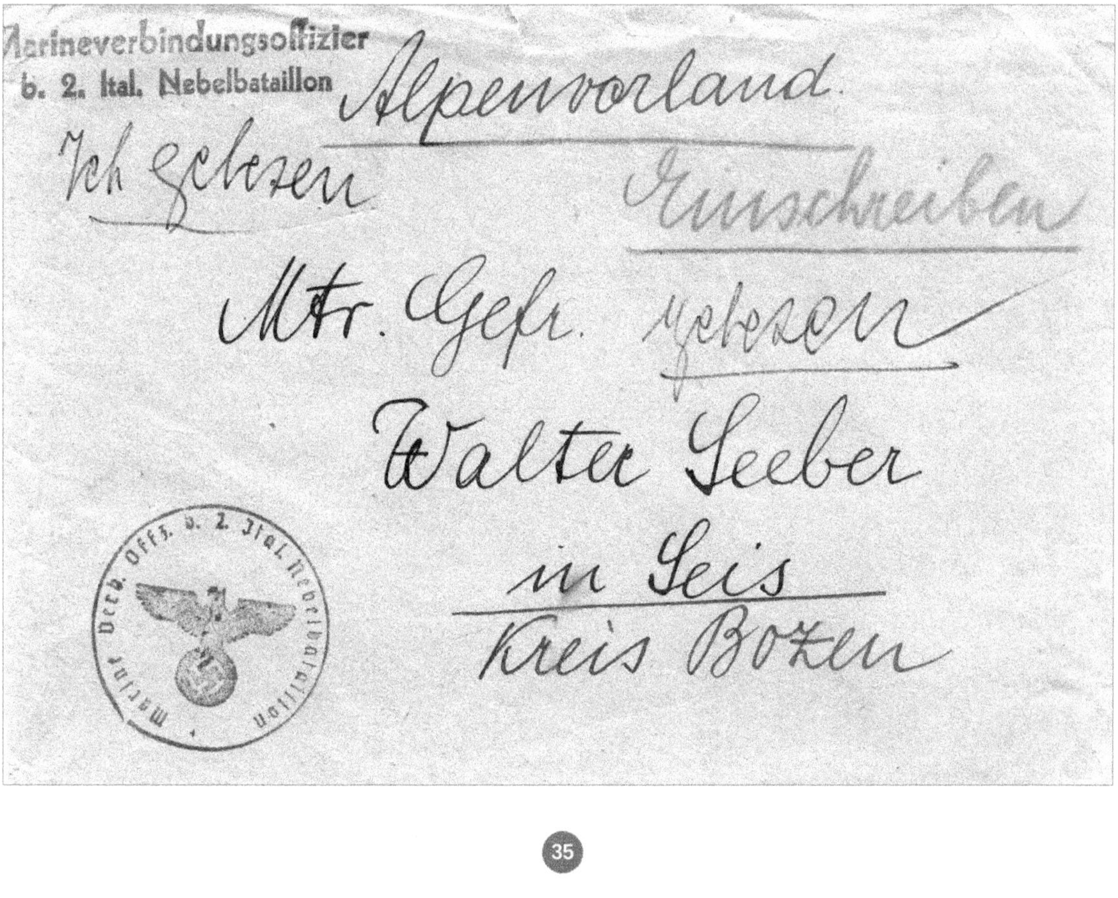

▲ Towards the end of the war, the 2nd and 3rd Fogging Battalions were also employed as simple infantry units. In the picture, some Nebbiogenians of the 2nd Battalion patrol the Baltic Sea coast in early 1945 (Pisanò Archive).

▼ Once the air raid alarm was triggered, the Foggings, put on alert, moved swiftly to the fog stations to conceal sensitive targets (Pisanò Archive).

▲ Close-up of one of the patrolling Foggings portrayed in the previous photograph (Pisanò Archive).

▲ The Fogging Geniers, having arrived at the prearranged position, lay down a chloridine fog curtain; they wear the protective rubber combination characteristic of their speciality (Pisano Archive).

▼ Picture of the Germans' route over the Baltic Sea: the front, as we have seen in the text, was also manned by the Italian Fogging Battalions, who shared the fate of the Germanic units in those difficult days.

▲ A Soviet officer observes some abandoned German armoured vehicles on the Baltic coast after the collapse of the Baltic Sea defence in April 1945.

▼ Plate by Guido Rosignoli depicting frieze and insignia of the Fogging Battalions.

▲ Fogging Battalion cap frieze.

▲ Fogging Battalion embroidered canvases (Riccardo Pantanelli collection).

▲ Reproduction of the insignia of the National Republican Army's chemical units.

▲ Drawing from the 'Provisional Instruction' depicting the beret frieze provided for the National Republican Army's chemical units.

On 15 February 1945, in the report sent to the Special Secretariat of the Head of Government by the Head of the Military Mission, General Morera, the situation of the fog battalions was mentioned, among other reports. It was reported that the Training Centre in Groß Born[12] had been dismantled and the personnel sent to Wilhelmshaven, where the Fog Troop Command and the 3rd Battalion were located, that the 1st Battalion was in Swinemünde and the 2nd Battalion in Gotenhafen, while the company stationed in Pillau would soon be transferred by sea, but without stating the destination. The report also mentioned a growing nervousness among the soldiers and some cases of desertion.

As the end approached, the Battalions were also employed in anti-aircraft duties, coastal defence and even as infantry troops both in an attempt to contain the Soviet armies, attacking from the east, and the British, coming in from the west, equipped only with light armament and a few panzerfausts, as individual anti-tank weapons.

Captain Di Pietro's 1st Battalion participated to the last in the coastal defence, to protect the evacuation of the civilian population. The very few survivors were taken prisoner by the Russians and, with other A.R.M.I.R. prisoners, were only repatriated in 1947.

The survivors of the 2nd Battalion, which was located in Gothenafen near Gdansk, sustained fierce fighting against the Russian vanguards, but managed to evacuate with makeshift boats by sea, thus avoiding capture.

The 3rd Battalion found itself, in April 1945, without special fog equipment and with a severely reduced unit strength; despite this, it was engaged in heavy fighting against British troops as normal infantry and surrendered, when the war was over, to a Polish unit.

No details are known about the end of the other two Fogging Battalions.

Thus ended, between the end of April and the beginning of May 1945, the operational activity of the Italian fog battalion sappers in Germany, which had lasted 30 months, started with the stars of the Royal Army at the lapel and the flag of the Kingdom of Italy and ended with the gladiators and the flag of the Italian Social Republic.

That of the fog battalions was a long activity that was little publicised in Italy. Carried out with self-sacrifice and a spirit of sacrifice, it was greatly appreciated by the German ally, always quick to praise the Italian soldier, who on this occasion, however, was able to recognise the professionalism of the fog engineers.

---

12 Groß Born is the present-day Polish town of Borne Sulinowo, located within the West Pomeranian Voivodeship . From 1945, following the conquest by the Red Army, the area became a Soviet military base, and excluded from Polish jurisdiction, until October 1992 when, following the withdrawal of Soviet troops, the town became part of Poland again.

HISTORY OF THE UNITS[13]

1. Fogging Troop Command

Location: Wilhelmshaven (Szczecin)
Feldpostnummer: 82665 (from 7 March 1944)
Commander:
- Major Giuseppe Calafiore
- Colonel I.G.S. (later promoted to General) Carlo Fedi

Administrative Officer: Captain Ruggero Altafini
Fascist Orientation Officer (U.D.O.F.): Lieutenant Primo Lavizzari[14]
Staff (January - February 1945)
5 officers, 3 non-commissioned officers and 9 military personnel

It was established in the autumn of 1943 and its command was entrusted ad interim to Major Giuseppe Calafiore; the actual and final commander was Colonel General (later actually promoted to General) Carlo Fedi; there was a Liaison Unit with the OKW. Of the personnel of the Fogging Troop Command, the Liaison Unit and the Training Centre, stationed in Wilhelmshaven in April 1945, there is no certain information: from some testimonies it is probable that they were involved in the fighting together with the soldiers of the 3rd Battalion and were captured by the Poles.

2. Fogging Troop Training Centre (Ausbildungstager)

Location: Wilhelmshaven (Szczecin)
Feldpostnummer: 82665 (from 7 March 1944)
Organigram (January - February 1945)
- Command Company
- 51st Company

Staff (January - February 1945)
48 officers, 38 non-commissioned officers and 171 military personnel

Stationed in Wilhelmshaven (Szczecin), it identified itself with the Command, of which it was, in fact, the Command Company.

---

13 The data concerning organigrams and staffing levels refer to the period from January to February 1945 and are taken from the 'Report on January and February 1945 Activities' of the Italian Military Mission in Germany, the only official document concerning the unit, which contains a staffing table, which has been found. Another organigram was presented by Giorgio Pisanò in "Gli ultimi in Grigioverde", a work cited in the bibliography, and is given at the end of the chapter, although it seems less realistic and it is not clear to which period it may refer.
14 Assigned to the Baltic Foggings in autumn 1944.

In Wilhelmshaven, numerous Italian Fogging soldiers participated in the construction of a large air raid shelter, which was to serve as protection for the population during bombing raids. It is unclear whether the Foggings employed were members of the Training Centre (more likely) or the 3rd Fogging Battalion, but it is certain that they were assisted by the work of numerous Italian civilian workers, 'taken' from among those who were in Germany as forced labourers. The bunker, which still exists today, has interesting and peculiar features. Firstly, it is very large and conspicuous in size and, for this reason, was built imitating the shape of a large residential villa, so as to blend in with the surrounding buildings (the bunker was located within the town centre). In addition, it was equipped with two entrances, each protected by appropriate guards, and two ventilation towers, which reproduced the shape of the chimneys of civil dwellings, built in concrete instead of brick. At the end of the Second World War, the bunker was not demolished, but rather, with the advent of the Cold War, improvements were made so that it could also be used in the event of a nuclear attack, which were never fully completed. Over the years, in fact, for inexplicable reasons, the structure gradually lost interest, until it was abandoned; on 12 October 2011, the bunker was donated to the municipality of Wilhelmshaven, which has been carrying out a redevelopment project since 2016, in order to be able to reuse the structure for social and cultural purposes.

3. I Fogging Battalion

Location: Swinemünde, at the Usedom Naval Base - Wollin

Feldpostnummer: 80178 (from 27 May 1944 to 13 July 1944) - 87688 (from 26 October 1944)

Organigram (January - February 1945):
- Command Platoon
- 34th Company
- 35th Company

Commander: Captain Raffaele Di Pietro

Company Commanders:
- Company Command: Captain Cesare Maturi
- 34th Company: Lieutenant Riccardo Magnani
- 35th Company: Lieutenant Giuseppe Ponzetti

Adjutant Major: Lieutenant Giosuè Cuccurullo

Section Commanders:
- Lieutenant Cinnamon
- Lieutenant Cafarelli
- Lieutenant Cressi
- Lieutenant Draghetti
- Lieutenant Ferrara

- Lieutenant Limberti
- Lieutenant Lippera
- Lieutenant Mantovanelli
- Lieutenant Miazzi
- Lieutenant Nerviani
- Lieutenant Pagliari
- Lieutenant Perlino
- Lieutenant Redanò
- Lieutenant Russo
- Lieutenant Sallustri

Medical Officer: Lieutenant Carletta

Administration Officer: Lieutenant Corposanto

Interpreting Officer: Lieutenant Carli

Battalion Command Officer: Second Lieutenant Lenarduzzi

Organic (January - February 1945):

19 officers, 29 non-commissioned officers and 418 military personnel

The 1st Battalion was formed by the Szczecin-based Fogging Troop Command in the spring of 1944 with specialists already in Germany and recruits from the ranks of the I.M.I., with a staff of over 400 soldiers, incorporating the 34th and 35th Companies of the 2nd Fogging Battalion, reinforced by a third Company, which went to form the Command, with soldiers taken from the Fogging Troop Training Camp. The command of the Battalion was entrusted to Captain Raffaele Di Pietro.

It was stationed in Swinemünde - Swinoujscie, at the naval base of the Usedom - Wollin islands, commanded by Admiral Lowe, a stronghold that had assumed exceptional strategic importance, due to the presence of the V-1 and V-2 submarine base and the bunker shelters of the Baltic submarine fleet. The task of the Italian sappers was to defend both the Baltic submarine base and the V-1 (Luftwaffe's responsibility) and V-2 (Herr's responsibility) missile launching pads, located in the far north of Usedom, in Karlshagen, from air attacks, with fog during alerts, at one of the missile sites directed by Walter Dornberger and Wernher Braun, the famous Peemenünde base. The unit acted in full tactical and disciplinary independence from the Germans and was only linked with the Usedom - Wollin naval base command through two Liaison Officers.

The 1st Fog Battalion also had its own periodical magazine, 'Il Saraceno', which was printed fortnightly.

At the beginning of April 1945, the sector held by the I Battalion was still free of the enemy; on these islands, the stronghold command had set up an imposing system of fortifications, for the defence to the bitter end of this last strip of Germany; numerous German naval forces, including several battleships and some Uboats, had come across the sea. In the weeks that followed, the 1st Battalion was so actively involved in the defence of the positions as the enemy approached that Admiral Lowe, commander of the stronghold, mentioned the unit several times in his Orders of the Day, finally demanding one last sacrifice from the unit: that of holding the positions until the evacuation of the civilians was completed.

In spite of the approaching end, when the stronghold was now besieged by the Russians and with the sea as the only link, the I Fogging Battalion once again received the inspection of high-ranking officers from the Republican Armed Forces Headquarters, being cited as the best fighting unit that had preserved its spirit of discipline, industriousness and aggressiveness, despite the distance from Italy and the contingent situation at the limit of bearability. At the same time, Mussolini himself sent a telegram to Captain Di Pietro, who also received a commendation from Undersecretary of the Army Basile. A few days before the inevitable collapse of the front, the commander of the Fogging Troops, Colonel Fedi, also wished to address an important commendation to the I Battalion, for its actions and courage, reported in the Order of the Day number 49 of 19 April 1945. Below is the text:

"BEHAVIOUR OF I. BATTALION

The I. Battalion, which had already been in contact with the enemy for some time and in difficult living conditions in na Piazzaforte Marittima, which was also violently bombed, performed well, recovering immediately after the consequences of the bombing and continuing its work, with the ardour and discipline that are its particular characteristic.

I commend the battalion and its commander.

I would like to remind everyone that in difficult times one rehearses characters and that it is not with displays of terror or personal concerns that one saves one's position when it is difficult.

Only with personal dignity can one maintain one's own prestige, that of the Army to which one belongs and that of our Homeland, which we always and at all times represent.

I REMIND EVERYONE THAT WE MUST NEVER DOUBT THE DESTINY OF OUR HOMELAND.

Carlo Fedi
Colonel as General'.

Following up on Colonel Fedi's praise, Captain Raffaele di Pietro addressed his own commendation to his subordinates with Extraordinary Order of the Day number 3 of 24 April 1945, which also appeared in the magazine 'Il Saraceno'. After quoting the words of the commander of the Nebbiogen Battalions in full, he addressed these words to his men:

"This praise added to the previous one and to the two citations on the agenda of the German Command of the Swinemunde stronghold, represents a truly unique privilege of our Battalion among all the neo-liberal units of Republican Italy.

Our activity, modest but precious, silent but not unrecognised, is thus once again rewarded with the best of rewards: the satisfaction of our Commands that reaches the heart and soul of every good soldier as the voice of the fatherland, generous and grateful for those who, wherever and however, know how to give everything for it.

To the commendation of Troop Command Nebbiogene, I add my appreciation for all my men in general and in particular for the Company Commanders and Post Commanders who, of all people, form the backbone of the work they are required to do and which they carry out with intelligence, willingness and discipline.

The I. Battalion maintains its combat post today with the same spirit, with the same discipline, with the same performance as yesterday and as always; for me, personally, it is a particular privilege and source of great satisfaction to be its Commander.

My soldiers: you have honestly and disciplinedly fulfilled your duty to your homeland, to your family and to our conscience. Whatever the fate of the war may be, you will return to your homeland with your foreheads held high, with the serene spirit of honest men and with the name of Italy deeply in your hearts.

With men like you, Italy cannot fail to be free, great, imperial as Destiny had designated it and as it really was until the fateful, infamous dates of 25 July and 8 September 1943.

Long live Italy!

THE CAPTAIN
BATTALION COMMANDER
(Di Pietro Raffaele)'

The evacuation of the civilian population could be considered completed in the last days of April, safely transported by sea to Hamburg, thanks to the constant efforts of the I Battalion's foghorns. The unit continued its strenuous resistance until the fall of the stronghold and on the evening of 3 May 1945, after having lowered its flag and destroyed all its equipment, it only partly managed to board the last ship leaving the islands, which were to be occupied a few hours later by Soviet troops, while the port facilities were consumed by fires and explosions. The 1st Fog Battalion was the last unit in arms of the Italian Social Republic to lower its flag, outside the national borders, on Reich soil. The few survivors were taken prisoner by the Soviets, only to be repatriated in 1947.

4. II Fogging Battalion

Location: Gotenhafen (Gdansk), with detachments in Gollen and Pillau
Feldpostnummer: 39626 (between September 1942 and 9 March 1944) - 87056, 83035 and 86402 (from 9 March 1944)
Organigram (January - February 1945):
- Command Platoon
- 29th Company
- 32nd Company
- 33rd Company
- 41st Company

Commander:
- Major Giuseppe Calafiore
- captain Lorenzo Altafini
- Lieutenant Pasquale Molinari

Staff (January - February 1945)

30 officers, 67 non-commissioned officers and 629 military personnel

The Battalion was one of two units sent to Germany in the autumn of 1942 and was deployed on the Baltic Sea, defending the vital stronghold of Gotenhafen in East Prussia.

In the spring of 1944 he handed over the 34th and 35th Companies to the 1st Fogging Battalion in formation. It was the last of the Fogging Battalions to take the oath to the Italian Social Republic on 22 June 1944, in the presence of the M.M.I. commander, Colonel Umberto Morera: only part of its members had been sworn in in February of the same year (probably, according to the documentation found, only the 32nd Company).

We also know from a document in the National Archives and Records Administration (N.A.R.A.) that the 29th Company was only transferred from Szczecin to Gothenafen on 29 August 1944, probably after completing its training.

Also from documents filed with the N.A.R.A., it appears that Gothenafen was protected by an impressive fog defence system in 1944. In fact, the entire area was covered by *'615 German and 72 Italian positions with ready-to-use fog machines'* (document dated 1 May 1944).

Due to the vital defensive task entrusted to the Battalion, the Marineoberkommando Ostsee had posted a liaison officer, Marineverbindungsoffizier beim 2. Italienischen Nebelbataillon.

In the last weeks of the war, the Battalion concentrated at the Gotenhafen base, by then badly damaged by Soviet air and artillery bombardment. Here, engaged as an infantry unit, it held its positions fighting hard against the Russians, together with the surviving German units, embarking to safety, evacuating by sea when there was no hope of turning the situation around. In this way, part of the unit managed to reach German soil, while others were captured, following in the footsteps of comrades from the 1st Battalion. A small part of Foggings from the 2nd Battalion, on the other hand, chose to hide among the civilian population, waiting for the Soviet soldiers to arrive. When they were tracked down, they managed to prove that they had not been in service with the Germans, but Italian soldiers who had escaped from the prison camp in the area. The Germans, in fact, made the soldiers of the Fogging Battalions use the mail address of the nearby lager to write home, using the services of the Red Cross to forward and receive mail. Thanks to this ploy, they were able to return home with the other Italian soldiers who had been liberated from the camps in the summer of 1945.

5. III Fogging Battalion

Location: Wilhelmshaven (Szczecin), with a detachment in Emdem

Feldpostnummer: 00448 (from arrival in Germany until 9 March 1944) - as of 9 March 1944 81226 (for Command) - 83684 (for Companies)

Organigram (January - February 1945):
- Command Platoon
- 38th Company
- 39th Company

Commander:
- Major Madau,
- Major Minetti
- Captain Vatrella
- Captain Barattini

Company Commanders:
- Captain Vatrella
- Captain Di Pietro
- Lieutenant Vaccari[15]

Adjutant Major: Second Lieutenant Bellinzona

Section Commanders:
- Lieutenant Sbarbaro
- Lieutenant Perlino
- Lieutenant Ferlito
- Lieutenant Borromeo
- Lieutenant Ferrara
- Lieutenant Mottironi
- Lieutenant Fracasso
- Lieutenant Lulli

Medical Officer: Lieutenant Villani
Administration Officer: Lieutenant Galiano
Interpreting Officer: Captain Pototschnig
Battalion Command Officers:
- Lieutenant Damiani
- Second Lieutenant Spinetta
- Lieutenant Cilia

Staff (January - February 1945)

22 officers, 39 non-commissioned officers and 477 military personnel

Together with the 2nd Battalion, the 2nd Battalion was sent to Germany in the autumn of 1942. Since its arrival in Germany, it was heavily engaged by the Anglo-American air force, which carried out numerous bombing raids on the naval base and surrounding areas in Wil-

---

15   The names of the commanders of the 2 companies stationed in Emden are not known.

helmshaven. The headquarters of the 3rd Mist Battalion was located inside Fort Schaar, an old defence structure dating back to the 19th century. Starting in 1876, in fact, the building of a defence complex along the riverbed of the Maade River along the north-western flank of the town of Wilhelmshaven began, a complex that was supposed to enable the protection of the town from a possible attack from the North Sea. At the centre of the defensive line were three forts, Fort Rüstersiel, Fort Schaar and Fort Mariensiel. During the Great War, the structure of Fort Schaar was later supplemented by a series of interconnected bunkers, which were to provide shelter at the main entrance gate of the fortress. At the beginning of the Second World War, Fort Schaar underwent further modernisation and became the headquarters of the Zentrale des Flakgruppenkommandos der Luftverteidigung (General Headquarters of the Anti-Aircraft Defence Group), although the fortress had already been used for these purposes during the Sudetenland Crisis, and from the end of 1943 it also housed the Command Headquarters of the 3rd Italian Fog Battalion. At the end of the conflict, the entire complex of Wilhelmshaven fortifications was demolished with explosives by British troops and the area was redeveloped in 1976 for the construction of a residential quarter. Even today, some rubble can still be seen in an area of the playground, which can be identified as the remains of the Fort Schaar casemates built in 1876.

In early 1945, it was the first of the Battalions to come into contact with enemy troops, being decimated and deprived of its fog equipment, which was destroyed. In April, the 3rd Battalion, under the command of Captain Barattini, found itself fighting as an infantry unit against the British. It was later transferred to a rear camp to reorganise, where, after more fighting, it surrendered, along with the German divisions there, to the Polish troops attached to the British.

6. IV Fogging Battalion

Dislocation: Fedderwardergroden

Feldpostnummer: 83035 (from 9 March 1944 to 20 December 1944) - 81560 (from 20 December 1944) - 19348 (28th Company from 3 February to 9 March 1944)

Organigram (January - February 1945):
- Command Platoon
- 28th Company

Staff (January - February 1945)

10 officers, 26 non-commissioned officers and 255 military personnel

Formed probably in the late spring of 1944, the 4th Fog Battalion was deployed in an inland area of Germany, in defence of industrial plants, probably chemical plants. In the above-mentioned report of 15 February 1945, there is no mention of the 4th Battalion, nor of the 52nd Autonomous Company. It is presumable that, due to the Soviet advance, the losses suffered and desertions, both units were disbanded and the personnel transferred to the other battalions.

7. V Fogging Battalion

Location: Zeit, near Leipzig

Feldpostnummer: 60482

Organigram (January - February 1945):
- 40th Company - Swinemünde - personnel 5 officers, 23 non-commissioned officers and 204 troopers
- 37th Autonomous Company - Emden - personnel 8 officers, 16 non-commissioned officers and 217 troopers
- 52nd Autonomous Company - Fedderwardergroden - personnel 5 officers, 20 non-commissioned officers and 177 troopers.

Staff (January - February 1945)
- 40th Company: 5 officers, 23 non-commissioned officers and 204 troopers
- 37th Autonomous Company: 8 officers, 16 non-commissioned officers and 217 troopers. According to a German report of 9 May 1944, it appears that this Company, at least until that date, was stationed at Gothenafen, part of the passive defence system of the stronghold.
- 52nd Autonomous Company: 5 officers, 20 non-commissioned officers and 177 troopers.

Established probably in the late spring of 1944, the 5th Fog Battalion was stationed in the German interior, in Zeit, near Leipzig, to protect vital petrochemical plants, which produced special synthetic petrol for aviation use. The 5th Battalion played a key role in defending these installations from a devastating British air attack, described by one witness as '*a veritable ocean of* fire'[16] on the night of 16-17 January 1945. In particular, the 52nd Autonomous Fog Company won the admiration of the Germans for the courage with which the Republican soldiers continued to operate their devices throughout the attack.

8. Women's Auxiliary Service Unit

Unfortunately, it has not been possible to find any information about the Women's Auxiliary Service Nucleus in service at the Fogging Battalions during the Social Republic. The few pictures suggest that there was a group of female auxiliaries at each Battalion, but the number is unknown (the only certain fact is that in October 1944 the 3rd Fogging Battalion had at least a group of 4 female auxiliaries, as they are portrayed in some photographs taken by the reporter of the Propaganda Operations Company Attilio Viziano during his visit to the units deployed in the Peenemünde area).

9. Organigram according to Giorgio Pisanò

In his work "Gli ultimi in Grigioverde" (see bibliography), Giorgio Pisanò presents a staffing of the Social Republic's Fogging Battalions that differs from the one found in the scarce

---

[16] See '*Fogging Battalions of the R.S.I. up to 3 May 1945 in Northern Europe*' by Remo Zara in ACTA No. 21 (May/July 1993), Historical Institute of the RSI.

official documentation found, both for the dislocation of the units and for the units that made up the various battalions. We report this for the sake of completeness, although it is obviously more reliable than what can be found in the "Report on January and February 1945 Activities" of the Italian Military Mission in Germany, although the latter refers only to the first months of 1945.

- **Fogging Troops Command** - Szczecin
- **Fogging Troops Training Camp** - Szczecin
- **1st Fogging Battalion** - Usedom Islands - Wollin
  - Command
  - Command Company
  - 34th Company
  - 35th Company
- **2nd Fogging Battalion** - Gotenhafen
  - Command
  - Command Company
  - 28th Company
  - 37th Company
- **3rd Fogging Battalion** - Wilhelmshaven[17] - Emdem
  - Command
  - Command Company
  - 38th Company
  - 39th Company
- **4th Fogging Battalion** - Emdem
  - Command
  - Command Company
  - 40th Company
  - 41st Company
- **5th Fogging Battalion** - Santa Hertagenhesch
  - Command
  - Command Company
  - 50th Company
  - 51st Company
  - 52nd Company
  - 73rd Company

---

17 Wilhelmshaven was the Kriegsmarine's main base on the North Sea.

▲ In Wilhelmshaven, the Foggings participated in the construction of a bunker, which was to protect the population from bombing. The bunker, which still exists today and is depicted here in a photograph from 1984, was built in the middle of the town and resembled a house on the outside, in order to blend in with the adjacent buildings.

▲ Civilians scurried to the bunker from the north-west entrance, disguised as a veranda, during an air raid in 1944.

▼ In a photograph from 1950, the imposing bulk of the bunker built by the Foggings can be seen on the right. It is evident how the outline resembled that of civil buildings in northern Germany and how the shelter could easily be mistaken for an ordinary private home.

▲ One of the bunker's two ventilation chimneys.

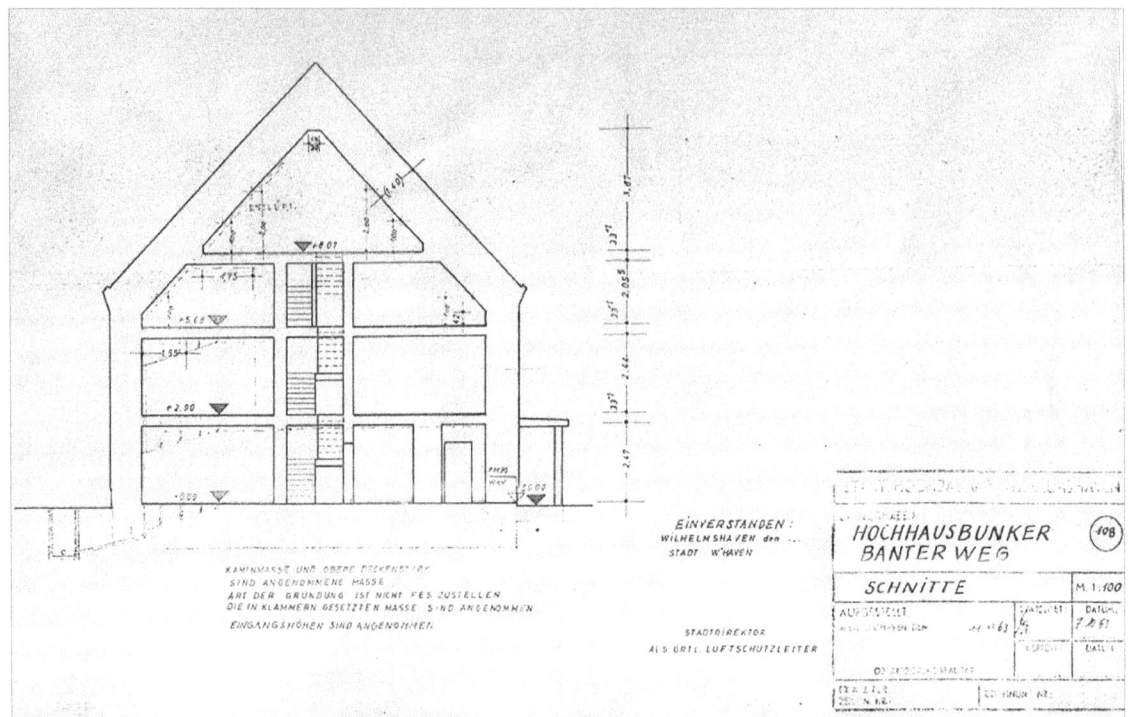

▲ Project from 1963 for the modernisation of the Wilhelmshaven shelter, so that it could also be used in the event of an attack during the Cold War.

▼ Detail of one of the air intakes on the ventilation stack.

▲ The access door to the bunker adjacent to the chimney in the previous photos.
▼ The same door seen from the inside.

▲ Fort Schaar in Wilhelmshaven in a wartime photograph.

▼ Another image of the Schaar Fort installations, photographed after a snowfall.

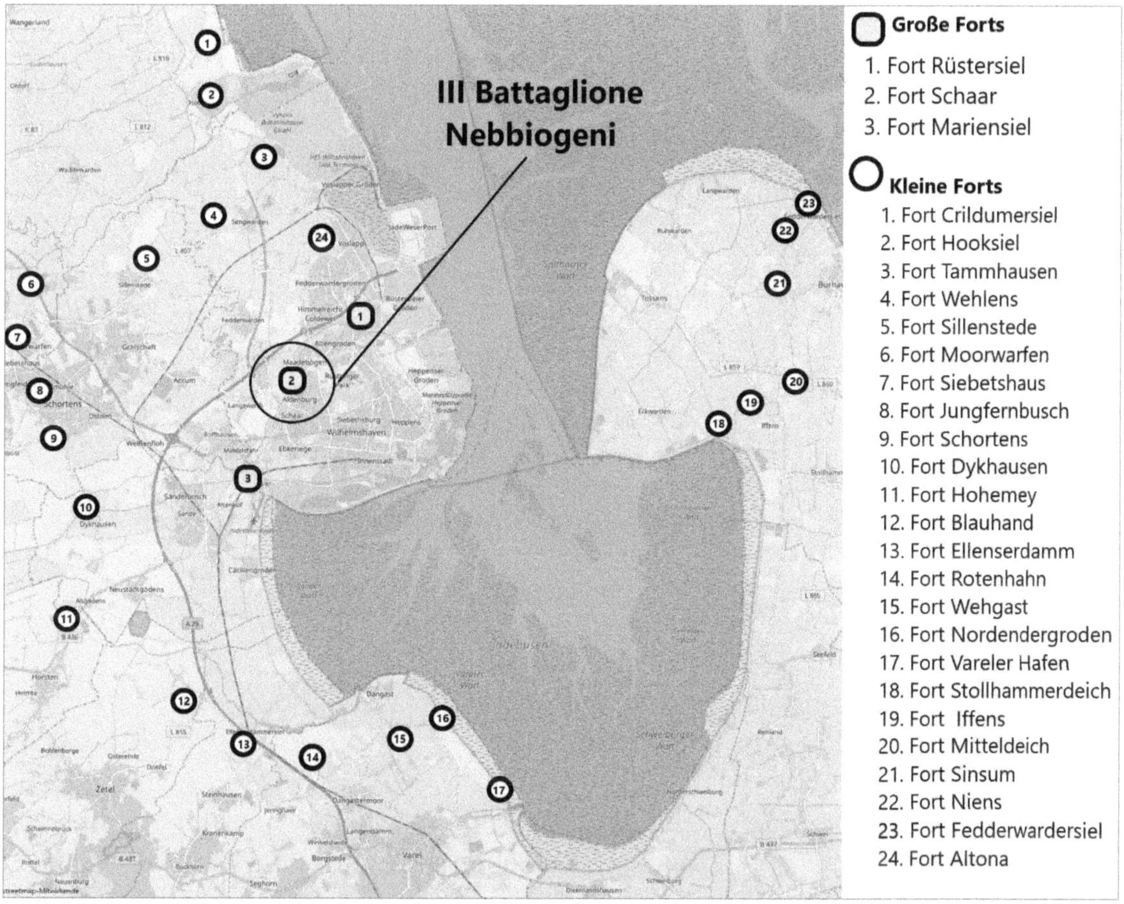

Große Forts
1. Fort Rüstersiel
2. Fort Schaar
3. Fort Mariensiel

Kleine Forts
1. Fort Crildumersiel
2. Fort Hooksiel
3. Fort Tammhausen
4. Fort Wehlens
5. Fort Sillenstede
6. Fort Moorwarfen
7. Fort Siebetshaus
8. Fort Jungfernbusch
9. Fort Schortens
10. Fort Dykhausen
11. Fort Hohemey
12. Fort Blauhand
13. Fort Ellenserdamm
14. Fort Rotenhahn
15. Fort Wehgast
16. Fort Nordendergroden
17. Fort Vareler Hafen
18. Fort Stollhammerdeich
19. Fort Iffens
20. Fort Mitteldeich
21. Fort Sinsum
22. Fort Niens
23. Fort Fedderwardersiel
24. Fort Altona

III Battaglione Nebbiogeni

▲ Map depicting the location of the forts of the impressive Wilhelmshaven defence system; the location of the 3rd Fogging Battalion Headquarters is highlighted.
▼ Remains of bunkers in the Usedom-Peenemunde area.

▲ Female Luftwaffe telecommunications personnel photographed inside Fort Schaar during the war.

▼ The ruins of Schaar Fort photographed at the end of the Second World War. As can be seen, the demolition of the imposing complex had not yet been completed by British troops, but the image allows us to appreciate the building's imposing wall structure.

▲ A stele commemorating the presence of the fortress, built between 1876 and 1882, was erected on the site of Fort Schaar. On each side of the base of the stele is interesting information about this impressive defence structure.

▲ Original postcard of the Territorial Fogging Division.

▼ Envelope of a soldier from the fog department. These cancellations are much sought after by collectors.

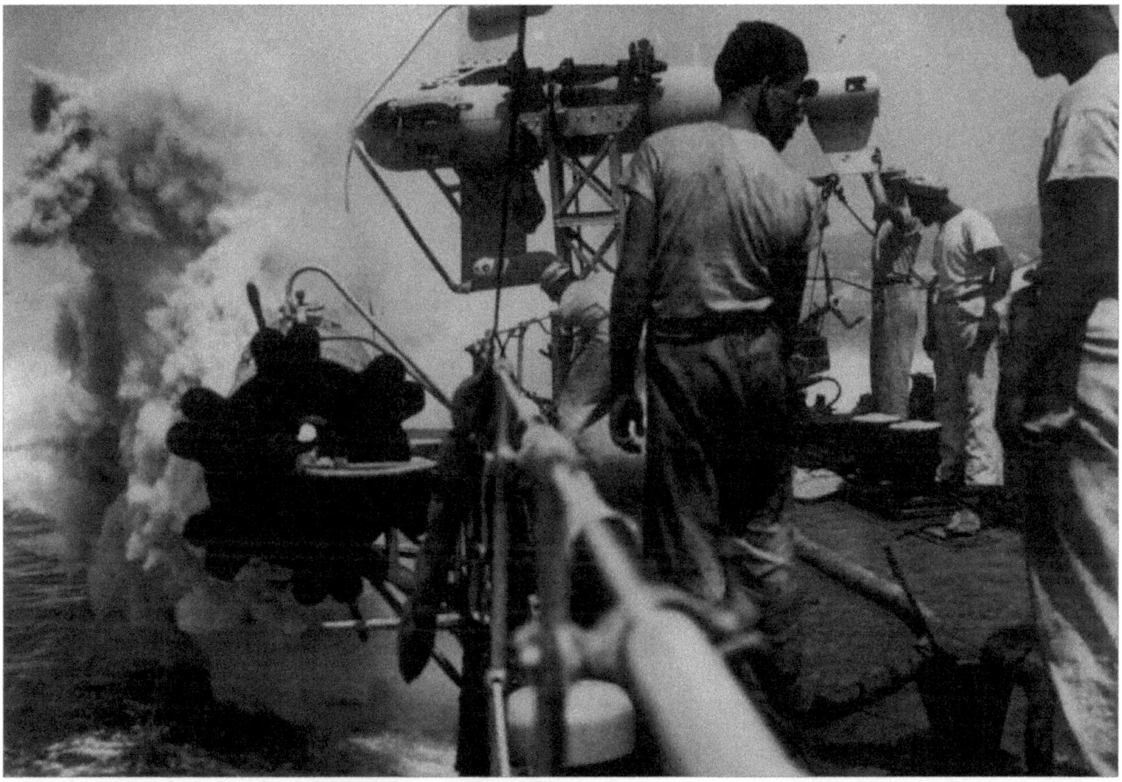

▲ Experimental fog units also operational on naval vessels.

▼ Wilhelmshaven was founded in 1869 as a military port of the Kingdom of Prussia. It was therefore of strategic importance in World War II. The relocation of the Fogging Divisions in the city was no coincidence.

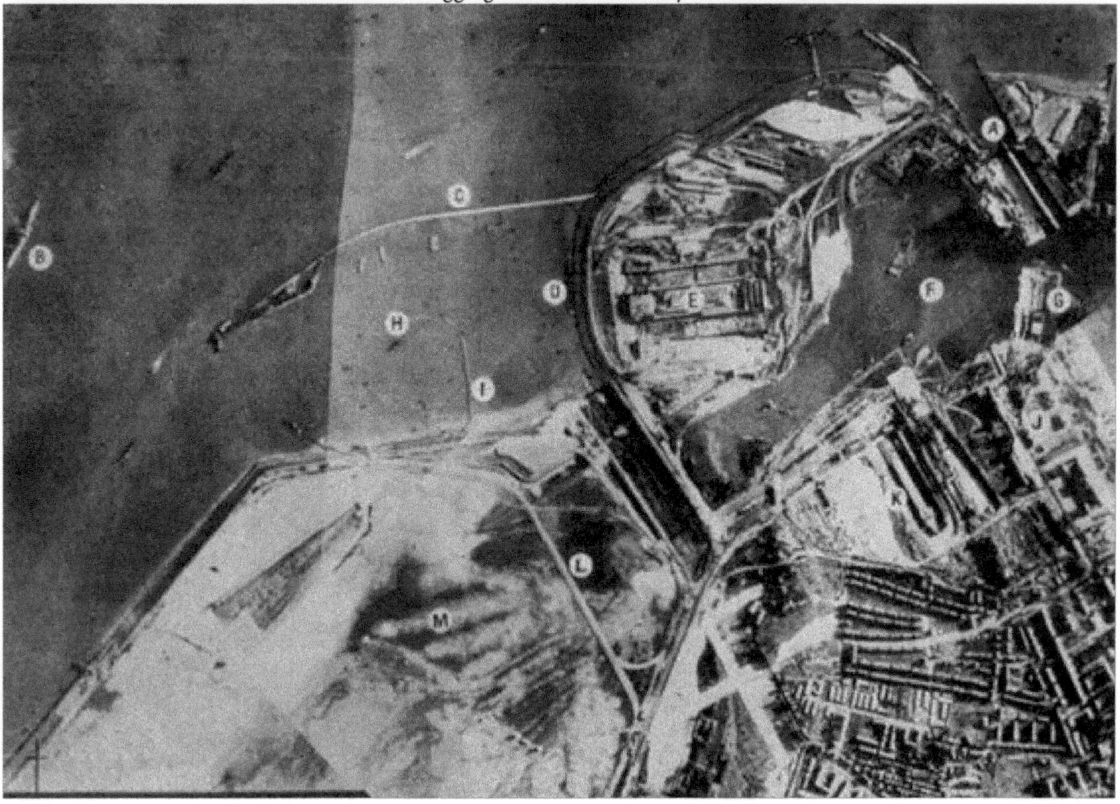

▲ ▼ Aerial views of the Allied bombing raids on Wilhelmshaven.

CASUALTIES

The following list contains the names of the fallen soldiers of the Baltic Foggings in the post-Armistice period. It shows a total of 70 casualties, which, for units so exposed to enemy offensives, is all in all quite small. On the other hand, it was not possible to find the names of the fallen from the period before 8 September 1943.

Fogging Troop Command
- Aldrovandi Dino, engineer, died 27 March 1945 in Gotenhafen
- De Benedetti Donato, engineer, died on 26 March 1945 in Danzig
- Tronconi Francesco, engineer, died on 17 April 1944 in Szczecin
- Viglione Pasqualegeniere, died 27 March 1945 in Gdansk

Training Centre (Ausbildungstager)
- Magnani Walter, engineer, died 17 December 1943 in Stargard

I Fogging Battalion
- Bassani Pierluigi, sergeant, died on 31 May 1944 on the island Usedom-Wollin.
- Bruschi Giovanni, sapper, died 20 August 1944.
- Burroni Luigi, engineer, died on 12 March 1945 in Swinemünde.
- Catellani Enzo, engineer, died on 12 March 1945 in Swinemünde.
- Fanetti Siro, engineer, died on 26 August 1944 on the island Usedom-Wollin.
- Favaretto Remo, engineer, died on 24 February 1944 in Danzig.
- Fernandez Giovanni, engineer, died on 13 February 1944 in Dresden.
- Franchi Spartaco, engineer, died on 24 December 1943 in Szczecin.
- Fraticelli Ferrero, engineer, died on 18 March 1944 in Szczecin.
- Fumi Cesare, engineer, died on 7 August 1944 in Szczecin.
- Gualandi Ildo, engineer, died 26 August 1944 on the island Usedom-Wollin.
- Engineer Angelo Maitti, died on 15 February 1945 in Szczecin.
- Mancini Francesco, engineer, died on 30 November 1944 in Szczecin.
- Mattesi Salvatore, engineer, died on 20 February 1944 in Danzig.
- Recalcati Giuseppe, engineer who died on 13 April 1945 in Stendal.
- Ripamonti Giovanni, engineer, died on 29 May 1944 in Szczecin.
- Tosi Ottorino, sergeant, died on 12 March in Swinemünde.

II Fogging Battalion
- Bardelli Remo, engineer, died on 2 February 1945 in Szczecin.
- Burrini Elio, engineer, died on 1 March 1944 in Memel.
- Calvelli Oscar, engineer, died on 10 February 1945 in Gotenhafen.
- Cannizzaro Francesco, engineer, died on 20 February 1945 in Szczecin.
- Casella Antonio, engineer, died on 13 February 1945 in Szczecin.
- Cavedoni Ezio, engineer, died on 14 January 1945 in Szczecin.
- Corsini Pietro, engineer, died on 16 October 1944 in Szczecin.
- Fornelli Ageo, engineer, died on 20 June 1944 in Szczecin.
- Fossaroli Primo, engineer, died on 10 October 1944 in Szczecin.
- Lauci Giuseppe, corporal, died on 30 August 1944 in Szczecin.
- Lobosco Italo, corporal, died on 24 November 1943 in Pillau.

- Longo Antonio, engineer, died on 20 June 1944 in Szczecin.
- Magni Giacomo, engineer, died on 19 March 1945 in Danzig.
- Paolini Renzo, engineer, died on 19 March 1945 in Danzig.
- Pasin Nereo, sapper, died in Berlin on 25 April 1945; he was a driver, probably in Berlin with the Italian Military Mission and had failed to evacuate with his comrades.
- Pastorino Fortunato, engineer, died on 20 June 1944 in Szczecin.
- Perini Gino, engineer, died on 17 April 1944 in Szczecin.
- Ranieri Nunziato, engineer, died on 30 August 1944 in Szczecin.
- Salvi Alberto, corporal, died on 12 September in Gotenhafen.
- Uccellini Elio, engineer, died on 19 December 1944 in Gotenhafen.
- Venturelli Carlo, engineer, died on 20 April 1944 in Szczecin.
- Zanoli Pietro, engineer, died on 31 March 1945 in Szczecin.
- Zumbo Pasquale, engineer, died on 30 August 1944 in Szczecin.

III Fogging Battalion
- Barbieri Marino, corporal, died 23 April 1994 in Wilhelmshaven
- Conedera Luigino, staff sergeant, died on 1 January 1944 in Groningen
- Garagnani Corrado, engineer, died on 20 July 1944 in Goerlitz
- Gerelli Pietro, engineer, died on 21 January 1045 in hospital in Brodnica
- Pacento Nunziato, engineer, died on 3 April 1944 on the island of Wollin

IV Fogging Battalion
- Baldi Fernando, engineer, died on 14 February 1945 in Goerlitz
- Coppola Giuseppe, engineer, died on 14 February 1945 in Goerlitz
- Frattaroli Davide, engineer, died 19 September 1944 in Swinemuende
- Laudadio Vito, corporal, died on 5 May 1944 in Goerlitz
- Lipera Antonino, engineer, died on 11 August 1944 in Oderthal
- Frattaroli Davide, engineer, died 19 September 1944 in Swinemuende

V Fogging Battalion
- De Angelis Agostino, engineer who died on 23 March 1944 in Goerlitz
- Facchin Elleno, engineer, died on 7 January 1945 in Przewoz
- Bramati Ambrogio, engineer who died on 7 September 1944 in Goerlitz
- Ghinassi Gino, engineer who died on 2 December 1944 in Goerlitz
- Gioia Tarciso, engineer who died on 11 March 1945 in Goerlitz
- Marzi Mario, sapper who died on 8 June 1944 in Goerlitz
- Villa Carlo Giuseppe, engineer who died on 28 March 1945 in Friedhof

Fallen soldiers whose Battalion is unknown
- Alberti Luigi, sergeant, died on 8 October 1944 at an unknown location in Germany
- Bazzoni Guido, engineer, motorbike on 4 May 1945 in Swinemünde
- Mussio Angelo, sergeant, died on 21 June 1944 in the Goerlitz Feldlazaret
- Olivo Guido, lieutenant, died 17 September 1944 Altengrabow
- Pollini Mario, corporal, died on 27 February at an unknown location in Germany
- Raffa Raffaele, sapper, died of hardship on 22 June while in captivity in Amersfoort (Holland)
- Wiedemann Carlo, engineer, died on 2 March 1945 in Szczecin

FOGGING DIVISIONS' UNIFORMS

The Foggings in Germany defending the ports on the Baltic wore the grey-green uniform of the Royal Army: a grey-green cloth envelope, shirt, jacket, trousers, and coat.

As chemical departments, they were also equipped with special clothing and protective equipment of various kinds (rubber suits and gloves, masks, goggles, etc.). A grey-green helmet was also provided, often with the chemists' frieze stamped on it in black. The soldiers also had one-piece fatigue suits, identical to those also used by tank drivers and mechanics.

After the Armistice, the Foghorns basically continued to wear the old grey-green uniform, but there was no lack of supplies of newly made garments, especially coats of a similar cut to that of the German Armed Forces, also in grey-green cloth. Protective clothing also did not change and the equipment already in their possession continued to be used.

A number of Women's Auxiliary Service Auxiliaries were attached to these battalions, who wore a grey-green uniform, consisting of a jacket, with a cut similar to a safari jacket, and a knee-length skirt.

On the lapel were worn insignia, consisting of a pair of friezes, made up of two crossed darks (brown handle and white blades) and five red rayon flames. Above it was placed the metal gladius, although it appears that, at least until October 1944, a certain number of soldiers continued to wear the Royal Army's stars on their insignia.

After the Armistice, the headgear adopted was the envelope cap, mainly the visor model, also for the Auxiliaries. The decoration of the cap consisted of a flaming grenade; the edge of the grenade was hexagonal in silver, the flame and body of the grenade in black, in the centre of the grenade was a silver cross. The whole was embroidered on grey-green cloth. The badges were common to all, officers, non-commissioned officers, troops and auxiliaries; only a few of the latter had the S.A.F. frieze on their caps, but the majority had that of the foghorns. The rank badges were those of the E.N.R. (worn on the sleeves and on the left side of the cap) and the S.A.F. for the Auxiliaries.

THE CHEMICAL SERVICE OF THE R.S.I.

The Corps of Engineers of the Italian Social Republic had a limited number of Chemical Depots: the Chemical Service Supply Centre in Asolo (TV) and the Chemical Troop Depot in Verona.

According to the Army General Staff report *'Situazione Comandi ed Enti Territoriali vari'* (*Situation of Various Commands and Territorial Bodies*) of 5 August 1944, a Fog Department was also in operation at the port of Genoa, with the task of protecting the important and strategic port, with a force of 22 men.

Chemical Service Supply Centre
Location: Asolo (TV)
Field Post: No. 845
Staff: 6 officers, 23 non-commissioned officers and 68 military personnel

It was established as early as 30 September 1943; no further information is available.

Chemical Depot
Location: Verona
Field Post: No. 857
Staff: 4 officers, 4 non-commissioned officers and 25 military personnel

Established on 30 September 1943, it was later disbanded and absorbed into the 27th Mixed Depot in the same city on 15 October 1944. The Depot formed units, deployed in the Adige Valley, deputed to the passive defence with foghorns of the Brenner Railway and supplied the complements for the 5 Mist Battalions of the Baltic.

TESTIMONIALS

Letter sent to the family by a recruit of a Royal Army Fogging Battalion

Interesting is the content of this letter sent by a recruit from the 2nd Fogging Battalion at the beginning of June 1943. The soldier, whose surname has been omitted for privacy's sake, in this handful of lines addressed to his family, expresses himself in an altogether enthusiastic manner about the new situation and the welcome he received from the local population, despite the distance from his family and Italy. One can, however, perceive how long the journey it took to reach the positions on the Baltic Sea:

"Feldpost, Wednesday 2-6-43

Dearly beloved, this morning - after traversing quite a bit of this country - I have come to settle in. I am fine; I am settling in to rest, which I really need. I am sure I will be fine in everything. You write to me immediately and always at this precise address:

Italian Liaison Office
W.T.S. Command - P.M. 145

Give me news of everything; I will write to you twice a week, if possible, three times. We are well housed here; everywhere we have found kindness.
But we started with potatoes!
I embrace you - Your Nino'.

Second Lieutenant Rodolfo Corposanto - I Fogging Battalion

Apulian second lieutenant Rodolfo Corposanto was an officer in the Administration Department in Avio (TN) at the time of the Armistice. Taken prisoner and interned in Gulag 132, a collection camp organised by the Germans in the Gradaro barracks in Mantua, together with two other subordinate officers from his own department, he was transported to Przemysl, in pre-Carpathian Poland on the border with Ukraine, as an Italian Military Internate, as he had not joined the Social Republic. In January 1944, he was transferred to the Mannschaftsstammlager-Stalag 327 in Nerika-Pikulce, and later to Stalag 313 in Hemmerstein-Czuluchow near Konitz-Chojnice in Pomerania, where he decided to join the R.S.I., following Major of the Chemical Troops Giuseppe Calafiore. After completing a period of training, Corposanto was sent on a four-day mission to Memel, on the Lithuanian Baltic Sea, to brief the soldiers of that Detachment's 2nd Mist Battalion on administrative management, and finally left Szczecin, as he was assigned to the 1st Battalion's Administration Service. The officer set up his office as the department's accountant and cashier in Heringsdorf, near the Ahlbeck seaside resort on the island of Usedom, the largest between the Szczecin

Lagoon and the Baltic Sea. He spent 11 months on the Baltic shore, which he described as *'pleasant and advantageous'*: with the help of Germans, he obtained a false certificate as a prisoner of war through the Berlin Delegation of the International Committee of the Red Cross, thanks to which he was able to send and receive letters to Barletta, then in 'enemy' territory, via Lisbon-Geneva.

When the Soviets reached Szczecin on 8 March 1945, he did not follow the Battalion's service units, which were moving westwards, nor did he stay with the Geniers, who continued to protect the bases on the island of Usedom, under attack from the east, but took refuge in the home of a local National Socialist sympathiser.

Having removed his uniform, he kept himself hidden in his hiding place, but was arrested by the Soviets a few weeks after the end of the war. He escaped imprisonment, however, by telling an improbable story as a prisoner of war, using the fake International Committee of the Red Cross forms in his possession as proof. At the beginning of September 1945, tempted to return home, he reached Berlin and, following the wave of the many Italian workers and fighters who, in order to save themselves, made a profession of anti-fascism before the American authorities. From the Stargard-Szczecinski camp for returnees, near Szczecin, he reached Italy and Puglia. Below are excerpts from his memoir, 'Fighter for the Freedom of Italy 1943-45', published in 1993:

"In the new location, my life changed almost completely. First of all, I came into contact with Italian military personnel (officers and soldiers) who had no idea of the vicissitudes and hardships that had characterised our post-8 September 1943, and in particular the period spent in captivity in the German Lagers (as concentration camps were called). For them it seemed almost as if 8 September 1943 had been a day like any other, so much so that for none of them had arisen the dramatic problem of joining the new regime in Italy, as it had presented itself to us prisoners of the Germans. Everyone, in fact, found themselves on the other side and in a new condition of military subjection without excessive trauma and I would say, indeed, without realising it. This could largely be explained by everyone's habits, by the interpersonal relationships between the members of the units and probably also by the friendships that had been formed with the surrounding civilian world, as I was able to verify in the following days. The adaptation to the new life was quick and smooth for me. To go from the bunk beds in the barracks to the comfortable bed in a single room furnished in a building that had all the characteristics of a peacetime hotel was something that went beyond all expectations, which naturally gladdened the spirit. Add to this the fact that this building, which was used as the headquarters of the fog wing, was located on the seashore in a seaside area of the Baltic Sea, comparable to our famous beaches in Rimini, Riccione and elsewhere, 5-6 kilometres from Swinemünde, where the fog wing was stationed, and you get a sufficient idea of the change I was coming to. The town and the palace are called: Ahlbeck and Haus Ostende. [...]

The command of the department as a whole was supported by a so-called liaison office, consisting of a major, a second lieutenant and two German soldiers whose task was precisely to link the services rendered by the Italian military with the German civil and military organisation. The two German officers spoke Italian quite well and had been assigned there precisely because of this.

After a few days of running in, I took over my duties cleanly and soon became accustomed to the new life. We were already in the late spring of 1944 [...].

While I was in Ahlbeck, we could send letters via another concentration camp located in that area. It was a trick devised by the Germans to enable us to have correspondence with families in the areas of Italy occupied by the Americans. The letters, in fact, travelled via the International Red Cross to which the families' replies were also sent by means of the forms that we ourselves sent along with the written letters. Obviously, there was the usual censorship involved, which is why we gave vague news, and it was only after returning to Italy that I then explained to my parents how things had really gone in Germany'[18].

Captain Raffaele Di Pietro - Commander of the 1st Fogging Battalion

"The Fog *Battalions had the normal infantry armament: in addition, they had special fog equipment (drums of sulphuric chlorhydrin - special overalls - masks - boots - etc.). The fogings naturally varied from day to day (and from night to night) both in number and duration: in the areas most exposed to the enemy offensive, an average of 3 or 4 fogings were carried out in 24 hours. Average duration of each fogging: 1 to 3 hours'*[19].

Lieutenant Attilio Viziano - Propaganda Operations Company

Lieutenant Attilio Viziano was a photographer operator in the Propaganda Operations Company of the Republican Armed Forces. Sent to Germany to attend a training period at the Heuberg camp, he was posted to Berlin, where he completed his training at the Propagandakompanie headquarters. From here he made a series of trips around the country, searching for Italian soldiers serving in the Wehrmacht. Viziano arrived in Peenemünde in October 1944, accompanied by a KP captain, and stayed for two days to visit the secret complex where the V-2s were built. He visits the factories built inside huge caves, dug by thousands of forced labourers and prisoners from all over Europe, and sees the launch pads with the missiles ready to be launched. He sees the thousands of workers forced to work inside the various factories in conditions of slavery, with the only consolation of at least having a guaranteed meal as compensation. At the time of the visit, Peenemünde had not yet suffered the deadly bombing that would raze it to the ground a few months later, at which time there was little damage from the Allied air offensive. He also takes numerous photographs of the interior of the secret complex, photographs that will be confiscated in Berlin and will risk costing Viziano dearly, but once the misunderstanding is cleared will be returned. He also came into contact with the Italian soldiers of the Nebbiogen Battalions, deployed in the area to defend the German installations. These are several thousand Italians who have little or no contact with Italy, whom some families now think have fallen or are missing in the great furnace that is the war in Eastern Europe. Viziano therefore offered to take care of sending the mail to Italy, a task he carried out as soon as he returned to Berlin. In his testimony, Viziano speaks of the presence of two regiments of Nebbiogens, although the documents cited in the text give the real number of soldiers framed in the Nebbiogens Units on the Baltic under German orders.

---

18 From 'ACTA' No. 72 (May/July 2010), Historical Institute of the CSR, work cited in the bibliography.
19 From a letter dated 12 September 1967 sent to Pieramedeo Baldrati, who was in charge of researching documentation for the famous multi-volume work 'Gli ultimi in grigioverde', published in the late 1960s by Giorgio Pisanò.

"My trip to East Prussia continued, and I made this trip because we had heard that there were Italian units in that region. And I found them: right around Peenemünde, towards Szczecin. These were two full Italian regiments, still wearing their stars (the CSR soldiers did not wear stars, they wore the gladius. I found these two regiments, which were special chemical regiments, i.e. foghorns, those assigned to create banks of artificial fog to conceal military targets (in this case the V-2 factories [...]), to prevent British and American planes from detecting their targets. These two regiments had been stationed in Szczecin since before 8 September: and they continued their work as if nothing had happened. The only problem was that they had lost all contact with the Italian authorities. I later learned, after the war, that these two regiments had remained in Szczecin even after the advance of the Russians, as cover troops for the retreat of the Germans, and had ended up (the not many survivors) as prisoners of the Russians.'[20]

Marò Remo Zora - 'San Marco' Division, attaché to the Italian Military Mission in Germany

Maroon Remo Zora of the 'San Marco' Division was assigned to the Italian Military Mission in Germany and found himself accompanying, as an escort, a number of high-ranking officers on several visits to divisions made up of Italian soldiers. One of them took him to Szczecin, where he witnessed the swearing-in of the 2nd Mist Battalion, the last unit to perform this ceremony on 22 June 1944.

"Baltic Sea, Szczecin, 22 June 1944. Under a milk-coloured sky, a grey-green lump, used, worn, indistinct.

It is the 2nd Fog Battalion of the RSI: 130 officers, 49 non-commissioned officers, 184 soldiers. A total of 363 men lined up in arms awaiting the ceremony of the oath of allegiance. The Armed Forces of the Republic had been sworn in, in Italy, since 9 February 1944, the anniversary of the first Roman Republic. Battalion II had not yet been sworn in.

High up on the flagpole, a large white - red - green flag with a black republican eagle seems to groan under the lash of the strong east wind.

In a dark charcoal Lancia Ardea, came Colonel S.S.M. Morea, head of the Italian Military Mission, and his escort consisting of an officer, a sergeant from the Autieri Corps and myself, a San Marco maro.

The grey-green lump comes alive, presents its weapons. Dry orders, the result of ancient habit, of lived discipline. The brief, meagre ceremony begins. It is strange to see, next to the grey-green lump, a group of Kriegsmarine soldiers honouring the Italian flag: only eight months have passed since 8 September.

Beneath the old helmets formerly worn by the Royal Army, men's faces can be glimpsed. Faces of southerners, worked by centuries of hunger and toil. Faces of Ligurian fishermen, of Romagna peasants. Faces of Roman bourgeoisie. Beards badly shaved by improbable razor blades. Faces of clean-cut young people, faces of old people hardened by years of war.

Before receiving the mission order on Szczecin, I did not know that battalions in arms of the Republican Army were serving on the coasts of the Baltic Sea, the North Sea and other inland

---
20 From 'Attilio Viziano - Ricordi di un corrispondente di guerra' by Bobbio Roberto, Cucut Carlo, work cited in bibliography.

▲ Officers serving in the Baltic Fogging Battalions, photographed in front of the barracks that served as accommodation in the Swinemünde camp. One can recognise, from the left, two second lieutenants, a captain, a lieutenant and a third second lieutenant. The variety of jackets worn by the soldiers is very interesting, above all, at the lapels, the distinctive insignia of the Foggings (g.c. Viziano Archive).

▼ Captain of the Fogging Divisions in Germany: this should be Captain Vatrella, commander of the 3rd Fogging Battalion at the time of Attilio Viziano's visit. The officer is wearing the brand new 1944 model jacket, the department's peculiar insignia and the frieze of the chemical department cap (g.c. Viziano Archive).

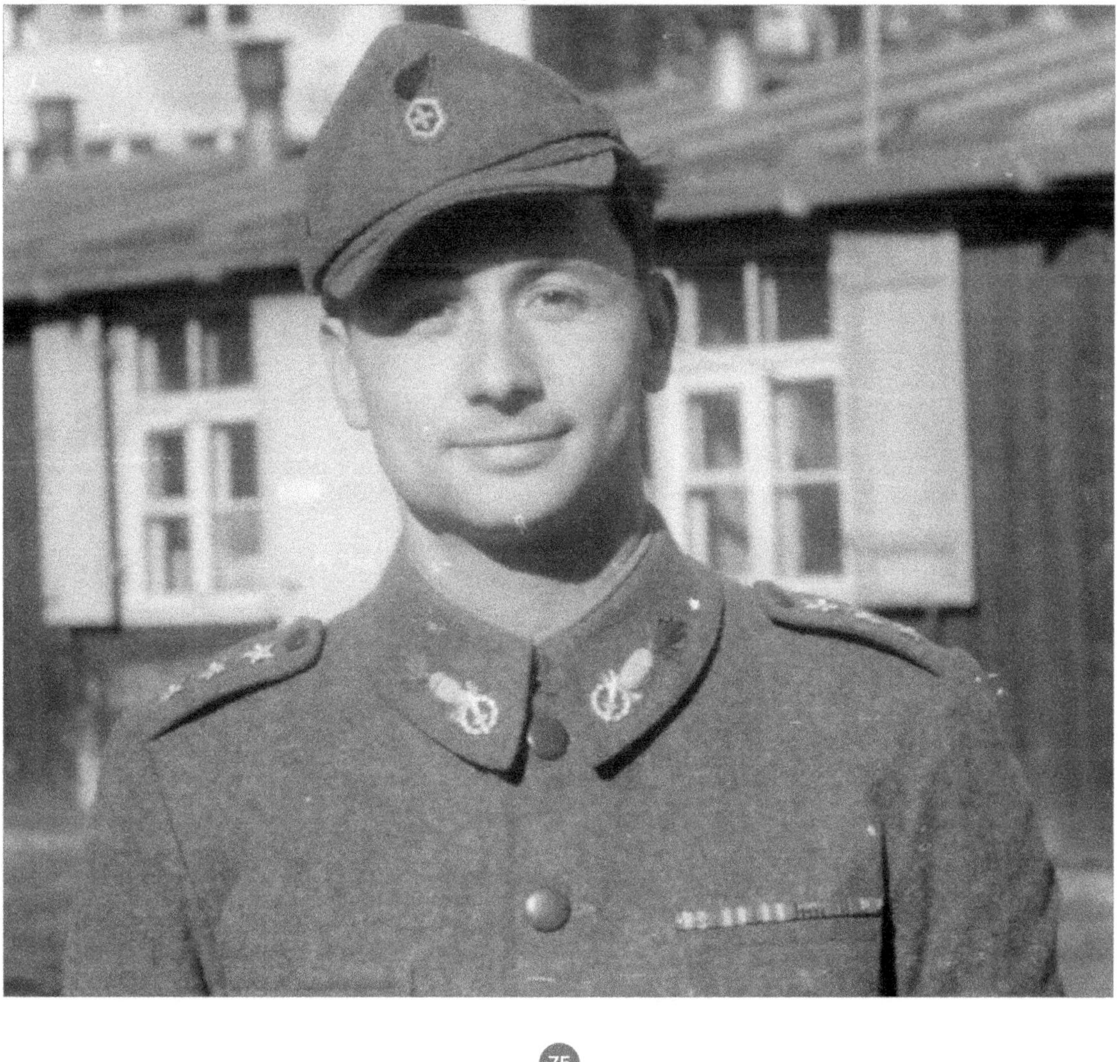

▲ A group of Auxiliaries serving in the Fogging Battalions: note that only two of them have the full Fogging insignia on their coats, while the others have only the gladiators (g.c. Viziano Archive).

▼ Group photo for these Fogging engineers; interesting is the mixture of uniforms adopted, which even includes one-piece fatigue suits. Behind them is a department truck, probably an SPA38R (Cucut Archive).

▲ Auxiliaries of the Fogging departments intent on collecting data from a weather station in Swinemünde (g.c. Viziano Archive).

▼ Reading the Italian newspaper 'Gladio' in January 1945 in front of the Fogging barracks in Swinemünde (g.c. Viziano Archive).

▲ Cover of issue 3 - year I of January 1945 of the magazine 'Gladio', the one in the hands of the Foggings intent on reading (g.c. Associazione Divisione Alpina Monterosa Archives).

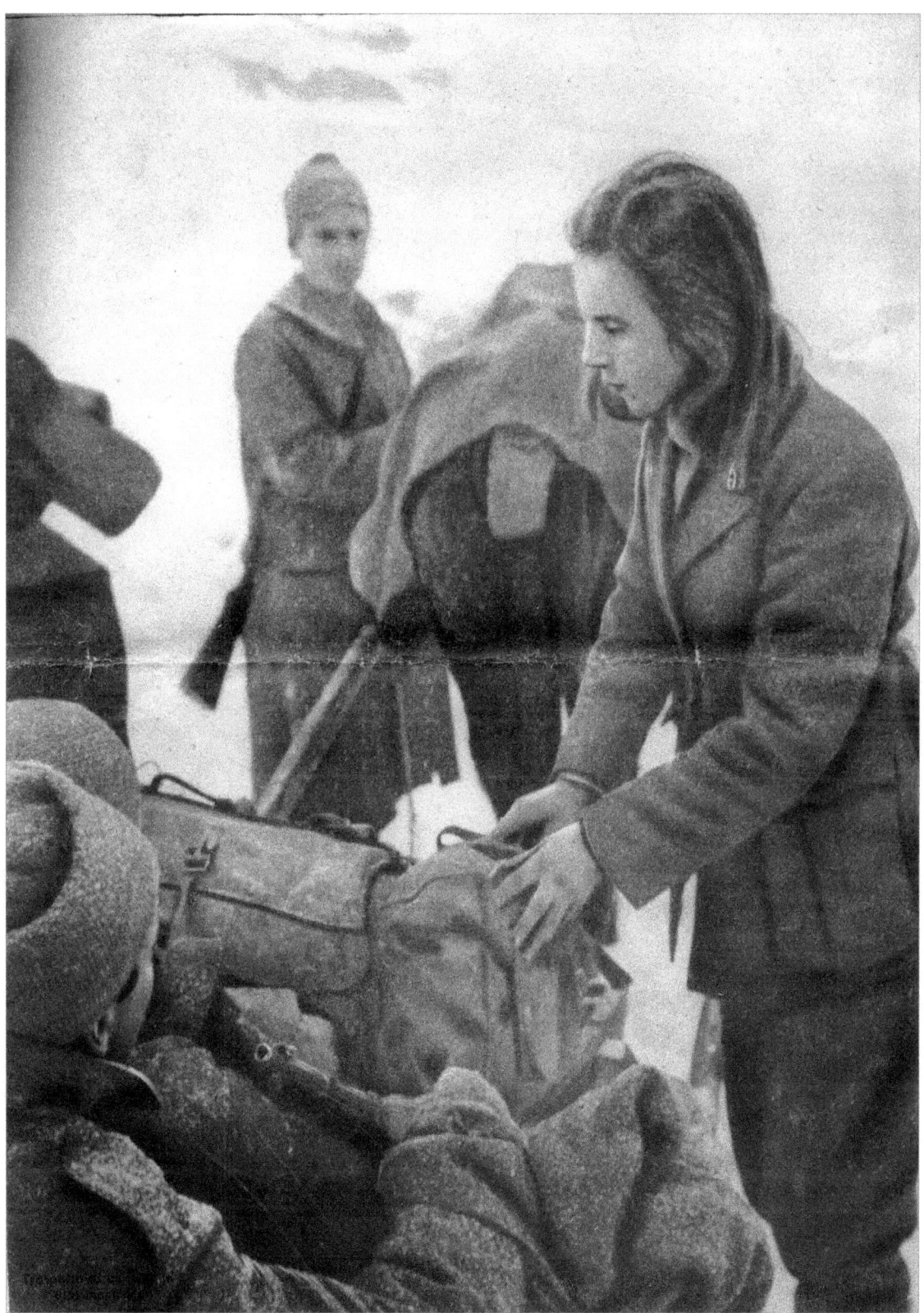

▲ Rear cover of issue 3 - year I of January 1945 of the magazine 'Gladio' (g.c. Associazione Divisione Alpina Monterosa Archives).

▲ Distribution of the ration in Swinemünde (g.c. Viziano Archive).

▼ Colonel Fedi's inspection of the 3rd Fogging Battalion in Swinemünde (g.c. Viziano Archive).

areas, protecting the most vital ports and industrial installations, destined for the production of those mythical secret weapons of which the newspapers spoke so much and which could, perhaps, avoid defeat.

Now that I have them there, in the flesh, before my eyes as an inexperienced and beardless Maro, I feel a sense of surprise. Rather than soldiers of a new revolutionary state, they look like young and old fishermen and peasants turned into Martians, with their boots that reveal - under the perfect protective rubberised anti-acid combinations - thick woollen socks full of holes and long knickers with elastic under the foot. Young and old fishermen and peasants, born from a stingy land, fed on olives and the toil of life, with slow gestures and long silences, in stables smelling of hay and cow dung, transformed into high-tech warriors, ordnance handlers capable of whipping the Bomber Commando bombers by operating, in less than 50 seconds, the deadly taps of chlorohydrin.

"I swear to serve and defend the Italian Social Republic in its institutions and laws, in its honour and territory, in peace and in war, to the supreme sacrifice. I swear this before God and the Fallen for the Unity, Independence and Future of the Homeland'.

The cry 'I swear' that gushes from the grey-green lump makes me gasp at its unexpected carnal power. It is a cry of guts, of blood, of memory that comes out of the breasts of those soldiers.

After the short, meagre ceremony, after a speech by the Chief of Mission and the Department Commander, the lines dissolve. The steaming ration arrives: potatoes, cabbage, beer, sausage, schnapps.

They are all crowded around the Head of Mission and his escort who have arrived in the strange dark charcoal Lancia Ardea. They ask for news from Italy: 'Is it true that the people are tired? What is being eaten? Does the government pay salaries and pensions to families? Is it true that there are people who, dressed in plain clothes, shoot soldiers in the back? Who will mow the wheat this year?". These are the questions.

Out of the frontier for years, specialists in a chemical warfare all coldness, calculation, daring and intelligence to be conducted with a firm heart and perfect training, highly appreciated by the OKW, one hears that, for the most part, they have not seen their loved ones since time immemorial and that they are especially hungry for Italy. Rheumatism and chronic bronchitis are betrayed by certain body movements or slightly too cavernous coughs.

I feel like telling them about the exploits of the Folgore and the Nembo, of Faggioni's and Marini's torpedo bombers, Visconti's hunters, Mussolini's bersaglieri and the legionaries of the Tagliamento, Barbarigo, Lupo and the other divisions of the Decima. I can't. I am unable to talk about our young volunteers fighting on Italian soil, under Italian skies, among Italians and perhaps against Italians, to these soldiers who have not seen this land and this sky for too long and for whom Italy is becoming, day by day, more and more unreachable and evanescent. I know I am wrong, but I just can't do it.

They refused the armistice, I think to myself. They have chosen to continue fighting thousands of kilometres away for a homeland that ignores them. They perform a service of the highest technicality and great risk. The fog that comes out of their sophisticated apparatuses is a deadly weapon of defence against the waves of enemy bombers that frantically try to destroy the strategic targets they defend. They are peasants, fishermen, factory workers from all parts of Italy, but they are capable of using cutting-edge technology and they stand there, like rocks, doing - for years - their duty. For the Honour of Italy. Well..., and I think to myself of those many gallant generals in Italy who are hiding in convents...

The days are very long in the north, during the summer solstice period. When, having finished the ration and the long report to the officers, our colonel climbs into the dark charcoal Lancia Ardea, ER number plate, it is now late in the evening but there is still plenty of light. We set off, in silence. The 363 soldiers from Szczecin are all at their posts. The RAF is always very active, especially at nightfall.

On the return journey to the Mission Headquarters in the troubled Postdamerplatz, I try to find out more from my superior, Sergeant Zangarini, about those soldiers who are so atypical and so different from the prototypes I had depicted.

"Tomorrow you will have to type a report for the Marshal's Office and that way you will know everything," is the reply. The next day, in fact, in copying the report I learn that other similar battalions are deployed:

- *on the North Sea in <u>Wilhelmshaven</u> (29 officers, 34 non-commissioned officers and 368 troopers)[21] ;*
- *on the Baltic Sea, at <u>Swinemünde (Usedom Islands - Wollin</u>) to defend the ultra-secret bases of the new 'V' weapons (26 officers, 23 petty officers and 340 sailors)[22] , and at <u>Gotenhafen</u> (near Gdansk) with 32 officers, 30 petty officers and 338 sailors)[23] ;*
- *to <u>Heydebrekk</u> (with 32 officers, 79 non-commissioned officers and 701 troopers)[24] ;*
- *in <u>Zeit</u> (not far from Leipzig) to defend vital petrochemical plants producing the very special synthetic fuels for the new fighter planes (6 officers, 17 non-commissioned officers and 228 military personnel)[25] .*

While, as a modest foot soldier, I am copying these figures, I certainly could not foresee that fate - in the form of mission orders - would grant me in the months to come the rare privilege and high honour of being able to meet almost all of the unknown heroes of the fog battalions of the CSR.

I could not foresee - as the late June rain drenched the craters of the Postdamerplatz - that from 17 to 21 December I would be sent to the island of <u>Usedom - Wollin</u> on the Baltic, to the I Battalion stationed in <u>Swinemünde</u> and that I would leave it under a blanket of snow just as the clouds of the Red Army offensive were gathering, which was then unleashed on 12 January 1945 (the I Battalion would only lower its flag on 3 May 1945 amidst the reddening of fires and the bursting of explosions, after having held its positions for months - in the face of the overflowing Bolshevik hordes - and having helped to rescue tens of thousands of refugees).

21 It is the 3rd Fogging Battalion.
22 It is the 1st Fogging Battalion.
23 It is the 2nd Fogging Battalion.
24 It would have to be, by exclusion, the 4th Fogging Battalion, although the location mentioned is a mystery. Heydebrek (today Kędzierzyn-Koźle) in southern Poland, was home to three forced labour sub-camps (E2, E153, E155) of Stalag VIII-B/344 whose prisoners were employed in chemical plants. In the (scanty) documentation found there is no evidence that any of the Fogging Battalions were employed outside German territory.
25 It is the 5th Fogging Battalion.

I do not even know that I would have spent the night of Epiphany 1945 in <u>Wilhelmshaven</u>, on the North Sea. Nor that - on the night of 16-17 January 1945 - I would be able to see in action - in an ocean of flames - the republican foghorns deployed in <u>Zeitz</u> as they defended from a devastating attack by British bombers the vital synthetic petrol production facilities - so essential for the new fighter planes - deployed there.

I open my eyes. I am in my Roman home. It is Christmas and I am surrounded by my loved ones. I am 66 years old, but the memory of those days, of Colonel Carlo Fedi, Colonel Trillini, Major Calafiore, Captain Di Pietro, Captain Altafini, Majors Mandon and Minotti, Captain Vetrilla, the modest, simple heroes that Destiny made me meet, is so strong that it has led me to write - so spontaneously and without any pretence - this simple testimony in their honour"[26].

As mentioned in the previous passage, in December 1944, the marooner visited the 1st Mist Battalion and, in January 1945, he undertook two more missions to the Foggings, the first to the 2nd Battalion, from which he reported these impressions:

"*On 6 January I left for a mission of the same kind as the previous one, at the 2nd Mist Battalion deployed to defend the Kriegsmarine base in Wihelmshaven, on the North Sea.*

The battalion to which I was directed had, more or less, the same strength (around 700 men) and the same characteristics as the unit visited in December. The days spent in Wihelmshaven therefore looked very much like those in the Baltic. Same daily routine. Same contacts with the Commander. Same evening conversations with the soldiers. Same problems. Same questions. No air warnings.

However, I felt that the atmosphere at that naval base was totally different from that at Swinemünde. In Wihelmshaven, one breathed a 'western' air, so to speak. One could feel the looming presence of the mighty British Royal Navy. Everyone was talking - very soberly, in fact - about submarine warfare in the Atlantic. It seemed that the U-boats had no future. One could smell, in short, saltiness and ocean wind. On the Baltic, a closed sea, it had been different. It was not the West that loomed but the vast East. Although the wind was, of course, also blowing from the West, it did not, on the Baltic, give the feeling of being a real sea wind. It seemed to come from the immensity of the Asian steppes. On the Baltic, it was not the British that one thought of, but the Bolsheviks and the American flying fortresses, their allies[27]'.

A few days later, in Zeit, the young man witnessed the massive Allied air attack against the German city's industrial installations:

"*After a stop in Grafenwoher, I headed for Zeitz, not far from Leipzig. Here, a company (about 200 men) of Italian foghorns was stationed to defend the essential synthetic petrol production facilities located there.*

I arrived in the late evening of 16 January, just as the historic air attack on the plants was beginning. It was the attack that would finally bring German synthetic petrol production to its knees. From that night on, the already exhausted German air force ran out of fuel and disappeared from the skies.

---

26 From 'ACTA' No. 21 (May/July 1993), Historical Institute of the CSR, work cited in the bibliography.
27 From 'Dentro la Missione Militare in Germania della R.S.I. - Storia di un soldato dell'ultimo Mussolini' by Morera Renzo, work cited in the bibliography.

The attack was devastating. A strong headwind pushed the artificial fog banks produced by our soldiers outside the area to be protected. The installations burned like torches. There were times when we found ourselves enveloped in dense oceans of flame. Several times, we had the feeling that we would never get out of that furnace alive again. With my helmet on my head and equipped with special goggles provided to me by the company's quartermaster, I watched, terrified and as if hypnotised, the astonishing spectacle. I looked at our soldiers. Calm and disciplined, they continued to operate their deadly but now useless equipment.

In Zeitz, there was no time for conversation. Brief words with the lieutenant. Exchange of information. Everyone was tense and silent. Nobody slept that night. Having delivered the message, I left immediately[28]".

Gianni Famigliano - journalist for the Republican Armed Forces magazine 'Gladio'

The journalist Gianni Famigliano visited the 2nd Mist Battalion in the spring of 1945 (probably between the end of March and the beginning of April), writing an article, which appeared in the 15 April 1945 issue of 'Gladio' and is reproduced here in its entirety, and taking numerous photographs, which accompany this volume. The description of the action of laying the fog curtain in an emergency, during an enemy air attack, which is minutely explained, is very interesting:

"*I had the particular good fortune to share many of the hard hours of siege with the units that remained in the isolated strongholds, witnessing the very special warfare, all coldness, calculation, audacity and intelligence, which led to a firm heart and perfect preparation.*

They had the delicate task of feeding the life and resistance of the strongholds located on the Baltic coast. Supplies to these large isolated bases constituted the most difficult thing imaginable. Each convoy represented a miracle of daring decisiveness, of timeliness of the Germanic Northern Fleet, which defied mines, torpedo bombers, Bolshevik submarines lurking in the Gulf of Finland and ready to descend from the south, the Soviet Eastern Baltic Fleet. And, darting with reckless and almost always fortunate bets towards besieged ports, it brought supplies there. The Italian 'Nebbiogeni' prevented, with their work, that during the ships' stay in the ports, these would become deadly traps for the convoys.

On the day I arrived in Gotenhafen, the old Polish Gdynia, after 30 hours of sailing along the winding trails of the secret routes, the battle against the narrow strip of coastline still in German hands had resumed in all its violence. A dark and rainy night, lashed by the wind, greeted me on arrival. No one on the streets of the port city: neither military nor civilian. It was now a territory that could not even be called frontline, but even across the frontier. The enemy, except from the sea, was squeezing all around by no more than twenty kilometres. Yet on the following morning I could see, as if by magic, life resumed as normal and almost serene under the opaque sky: the city services were running normally and the trains were still running within the tiny coastal strip, so that two days later I myself could reach Danzig where a spectacle awaited me that I will never forget. Within the immense surrounding ruins, I found the city from which the war raged completely intact with its illuminated and pierced houses, its streets decorated like scenery.

---

28 From 'Dentro la Missione Militare in Germania della R.S.I. - Storia di un soldato dell'ultimo Mussolini' by Morera Renzo, work cited in the bibliography.

A legend wandered in those days about its now collapsed towers, a prophecy, which the facts of these days have disproved, that could have been the story of tomorrow's world.

My encounter with the mists took place the other night and so much touched them in those contingencies and at those times that, through the dense telephone network necessarily linking the interminable theory of the various nuclei, the news was immediately transmitted to the entire battalion. Displaced in hundreds of admirably equipped cottages (many of them made up of suitably adapted first-class railway wagons) and located near the ordnance from which the mists emanated, the Italians were arranged along the periphery, constituting a very special defence belt: without ramparts and without trenches. Because of the small size of the territory, there was no time to give advance warning: it was the very breaking of enemy aircraft that mobilised the defence. The action of the foghorns therefore had to be lightning fast, as I saw it unfold in 50 seconds, without our soldiers even bothering to put on their rubber combinations to save themselves from the spraying acids, without even bothering to put on their gloves to adjust the chlorhydrin taps. Then, while the white cloak stretched out to safeguard the supply ships in the harbour, they stood cold and attentive by their ordnance, unconcerned about the rain of bombs, following the sudden changes in the wind and the slightest alterations in temperature in order to regulate this capricious vapour, which could otherwise, at any moment, betray them. Last February, the Italian foghorns at Gotenhafen received high praise for an action, the extent of which could only be made known at the end of the war.

Their commanding general, the commander of all Italian fogeys in Germany, wanted to visit them at the decisive hour to bring them in person the greeting and the voice of the Fatherland. And the commander's gesture was moving.

"It's time for the test," he told them, "you have to make Italy look good. Nothing else. But these were men capable of understanding certain deliveries without great phrases, as when on 8 September '43 they said nothing about their future behaviour, but the following morning they ran, without a moment's hesitation, to their fog-spewing bombs. So, in the imminence of danger, having emptied the last canisters, they took up their machine guns and positioned themselves alongside the valiant Allied fighters in the positions that they had largely built themselves, alternating the hours of guarding the devices and machines with those of working in the trenches.

In front of their positions they had seen in the previous days endless throngs of entire populations marching westwards. Ever-changing and exasperatingly renewing columns of German and, more significantly, Polish peoples fleeing before the Bolsheviks. And so one morning, in front of their positions, the foghorns also saw other men in grey-green appear: their comrades from the Pillau base who, having completed their task, having destroyed the installations, had fought their way through the Soviet troops on the frozen sea, had reached Gotenhafen and were then continuing westwards.

But one day the furious wave hit them too, and they waited for it at the very threshold of civilisation. In his visit, the general had asked if anyone did not consider their health incapable of facing the great struggle. He could, albeit with enormous difficulty, have taken someone out of the circle, where they were still fighting in another unit, also deployed on the Baltic front, but everyone stayed. And I will never forget, in the tenuous darkness of the Baltic night, the hands of two auxiliaries (although they remained up there with two of their brothers whom they had wanted to join at all costs in a fourfold solidarity of heart), I will never forget the hands of those two heroic Italian girls who greeted us waving their handkerchiefs.

Now other fog units are still on the eastern front; when the canisters are exhausted, when the scorching breath of battle approaches their faces, they too will abandon their ordnance and take up arms. They have not entrusted me, these men, whom I left on the extreme shores of western civilisation to share with the German fighters the lofty task of defending the heart of Europe, with any particular message. "God protect the homeland, God help the brothers fighting on the fronts of Italy. This message I bring to those who on the Alps and Apennines today fight with the same heart as those I left up there on the shores of the Baltic"[29].

---

29 From 'Gli ultimi in Grigioverde' by Giorgio Pisanò, work cited in the bibliography.

DOCUMENTS

MEMORIA

PER L'ADDESTRAMENTO DEI QUADRI E DELLE UNITA' NEBBIOGENE ITALIANE IMPIEGATE NEL L'AMBITO DELLA MARINA DA GUERRA GERMANICA

−o−o−o−

▲ Title page of the manual for Nebbiogens written by Major Calafiore. Entitled 'Memoir for the Training of Italian Fog Troops and Fog Units Employed in the German Navy', it was a text classified at the time as 'Secret', which systematised the employment of fog troops in that particular theatre, according to the doctrines of the 1940s, providing an operational guide on the organisation of the fogging of military targets, to be distributed to the Foggings and Kriegsmarine soldiers during the training course held at the Fog Troop Training Centre in Szczecin (Acta Archive).

▲ Diagram of the deployment of a Fog Battalion, with Italian equipment, to be deployed in

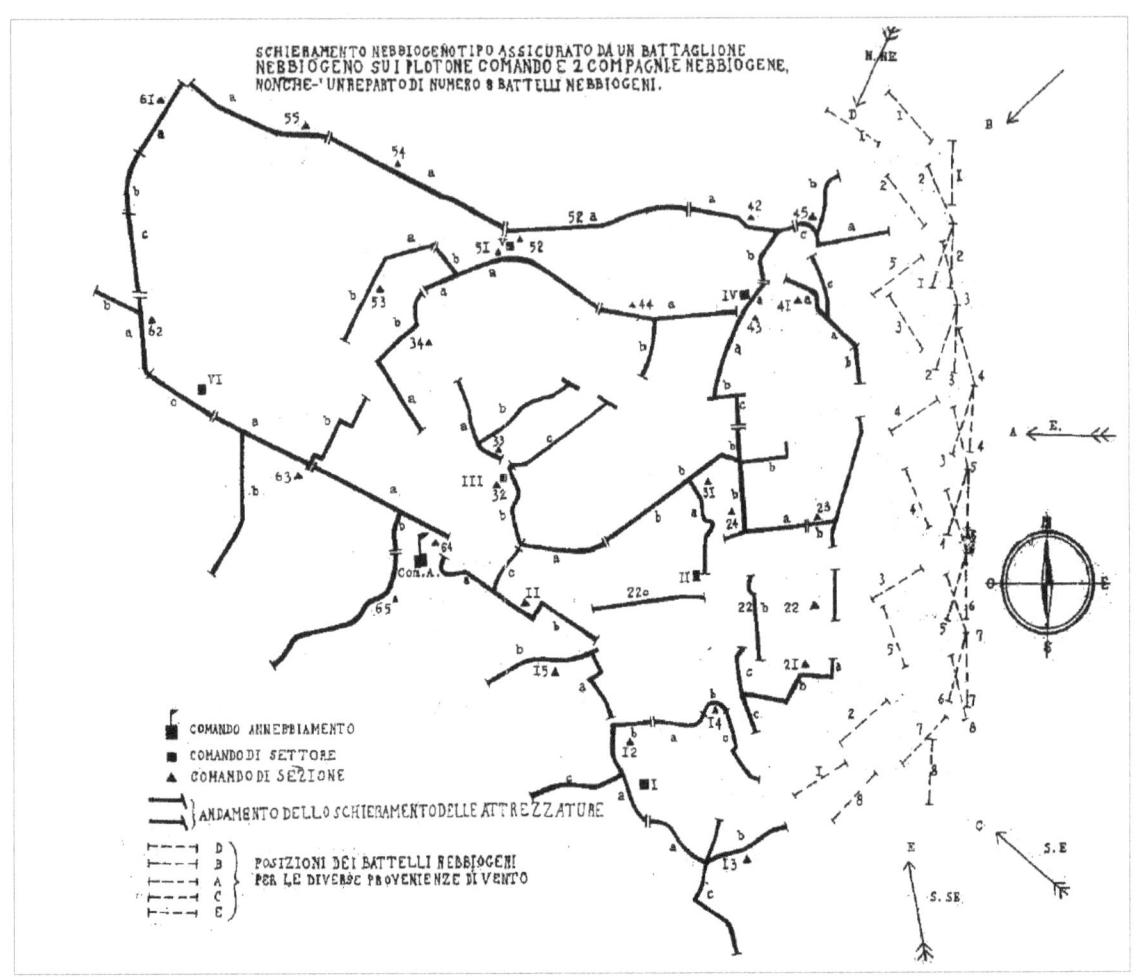

the event of an enemy attack, extracted from the manual written by Major Calafiore. The deployment was evidently designed on the basis of experience in the Baltic, as it envisaged the presence of both operational nuclei ashore and operational nuclei at sea. In fact, in addition to the entire battalion, articulated on Command Platoon and 2 Fog Companies, the deployment of 8 fog boats was planned, which were to support the passive defence, fogging from the water. The study turns out to be extremely meticulous and accurate: it indicates how the individual elements of the chemical unit should be positioned, according to the different possible wind directions (Acta Archive).

▶ Interesting document from the Italian Military Mission in Germany, concerning the 2nd Mist Battalion. It is the personal file of a corporal from the 32nd Company of the 2nd Battalion Nebbiogen, useful for the payment of war allowances. The card shows that the soldier, recalled to service in 1942, had been assigned to the 2nd Foghorn Battalion in August 1942 and, following the Armistice, had decided to continue fighting alongside the Germans, later joining the Italian Social Republic, still with the 2nd Foghorn, stationed in Gotenhafen, taking the oath in front of the Battalion commander, Major Giuseppe Calafiore, on 10 February 1944 (private collection).

MISSIONE MILITARE ITALIANA IN GERMANIA

II. BATTAGLIONE NEBBIOGENO

Scheda personale per il pagamento dell'indennita' di guerra o dell'assistenza alla famiglia ai sensi del Decreto 1/11/43 XXII del Capo dello Stato.

Cap.le. Magg.

(1) Ciancagli (2) Ottavio (3) fu Antonio

nato a (4) Foiano della Chiana provincia di Arezzo (5) 24/3/20

(6) Cap.le. Magg. (7) Richiamato il (8) _____

Ha prestato effettivo servizio col suddetto grado dal (9) 15/6/42 alla 32 Comp. Nebb. II Btg.

Il 9/9/43 e' rimasto in continuazione di servizio con la (10) 32 Comp. Nebb. del II Btg. Nebb. dislocata per l'annebbiamento del porto di (11) GOTENHAFEN (Germania), quale (12) _____

Detto corpo aveva per centro di mobilitazione il (13) Rgt. A. Roma

Il sottoscritto e' stato soddisfatto degli assegni previsti dal precedente trattamento economico fino a tutto il (14) 31 Ottobre 1943 dall'amm.ne del II. Btg. Nebb. Alla data del 1 febbraio 1944 XXII egli prestava servizio presso il (16) II Btg. Nebb. quale (12) _____

Si e' arruolato nelle FF. AA. della Repubblica Sociale Italiana il (17) 9 Settembre 1943 ed ha prestato giuramento il (5) 10 Febbraio 1944 alla presenza del (18) Com.te di Btg.

E' insignito delle seguenti decorazioni al valor militare (19) di cui mantiene il godimento della pensione e soprassoldo annessovi (20) _____

---

(1) Cognome — (2) Nome — (3) Paternita' — (4) Comune — (5) Giorno, mese, anno — (6) Grado militare rivestito nelle FF. AA. regie l'8/9 1943 XXI — (7) Categoria: S. P. E., riserva, complemento, ecc. — (8) Anzianita' di grado — (9) Indicare i singoli periodi di servizio ed il corpo presso il quale si sono prestati (per i soli militari delle categorie in congedo aventi grado inferiore a quello di Ten. Colonnello) — (10) Compagnia nebbiogena cui era effettivo — (11) Base navale d'impiego — (12) Carica ricoperta — (13) Deposito o Distretto Militare od altro ente territoriale che aveva la matricola degli effettivi del corpo mobilitato — (14) data — (15) Corpo che ha pagato gli assegni — (16) Corpo — (17) Data apposta sulla scheda di adesione da ciascuno sottoscritta a suo tempo — (18) Carica di chi ha presieduto alla funzione del giuramento e che ha firmato il relativo atto (per i soli Ufficiali e Sottufficiali) — (19) Compreso l'Ordine Militare di Savoia — (20) Nell'ordine cronologico, con la specificazione del fatto d'armi e la data di esso risultante al termine della motivazione.

▲ Document from the Fogging Training Centre on the taking into service of an Italian soldier in August 1944 (https://miles.forumcommunity.net/?t=62412956&st=15).

▶ Excerpt from the 'Report on January and February 1945 Activities' of the Italian Military Mission in Germany, which summarises the strength and deployment of the Baltic Mist Battalions at the beginning of 1945. The Battalions are described in enthusiastic words within the Report:
"*NEBBIOGEN REPARTS: speciality of the Engineer Chemical Section of skilful, daring and much-needed assistance first to the German Navy and then to all the major bases*".

▶ Interesting Feldpost envelope, sent to his family in Italy by a sergeant of the 2nd Feldpost Battalion on 27 February 1944. The sender indicated Feldpostnummer 39626, which was in force for the 2nd Battalion until the beginning of March 1944. The family and military details on the missive have been deliberately obscured (private collection).

d) Reparti Nebbiogeni

Reparti	Dislocazione	Forza effettiva Uff.	Sott.	Trup.	Totale
Com.truppe nebbiogene e Nucleo Coll. con l'OKM	Wilhelmshafen	5	3	9	17
Campo addestramento - Cp. Com. e 51^ cp.	"	48	38	171	257
I^ BTG (pl.com. - 34^Cp. e 35^Cp.).	Swinemünde	19	29	418	466
II^ BTG (pl.com. - 29^Cp. 32^Cp. - 33^Cp. - 41^ Cp.)	Gotenhafen	30	67	629	726
III^ BTG (pl.com. - 38^ Cp. 39^ Cp.).	Wilhelmshafen	22	39	477	538
IV^ BTG (pl.com. - 28^ Cp.)	Fedderwardergroden	10	26	225	261
40^ Cp.	Swinemünde	5	23	204	232
37^ Cp. autonoma	Emden	8	16	217	241
52^ Cp. autonoma	Fedderwardergroden	5	20	177	202
TOTALE		154	261	2.527	2.942

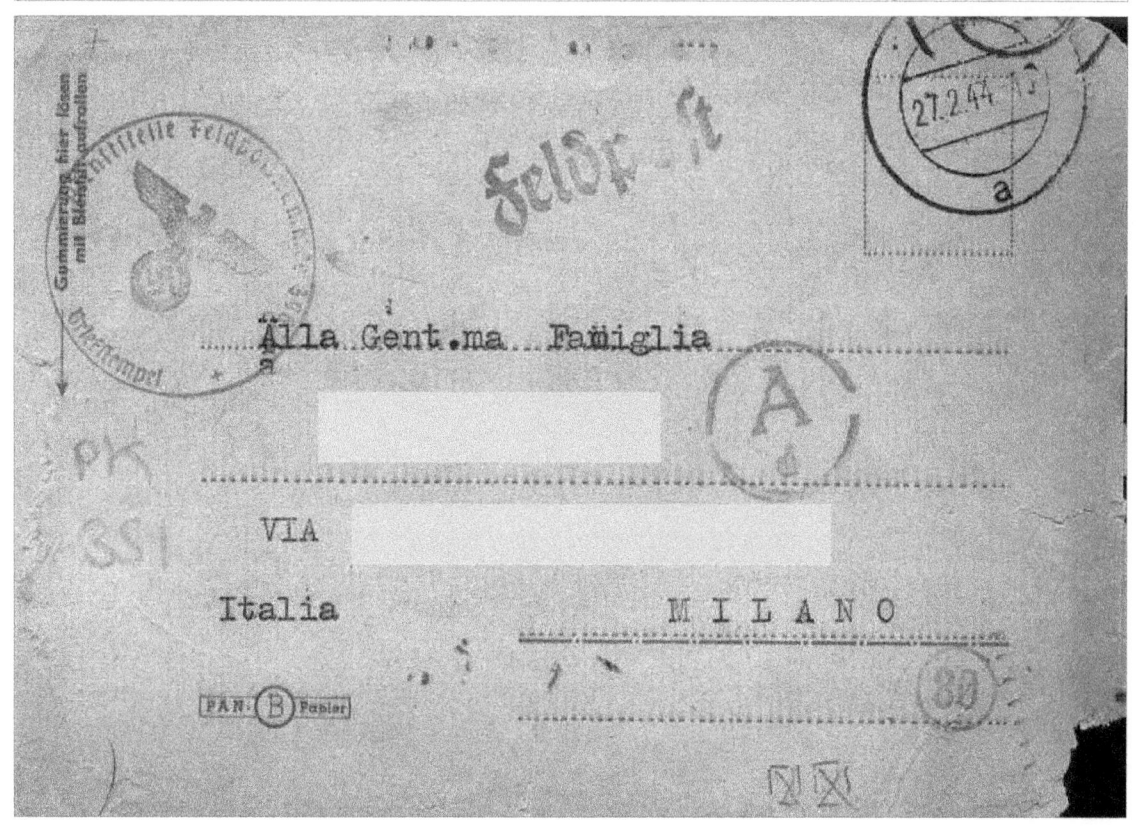

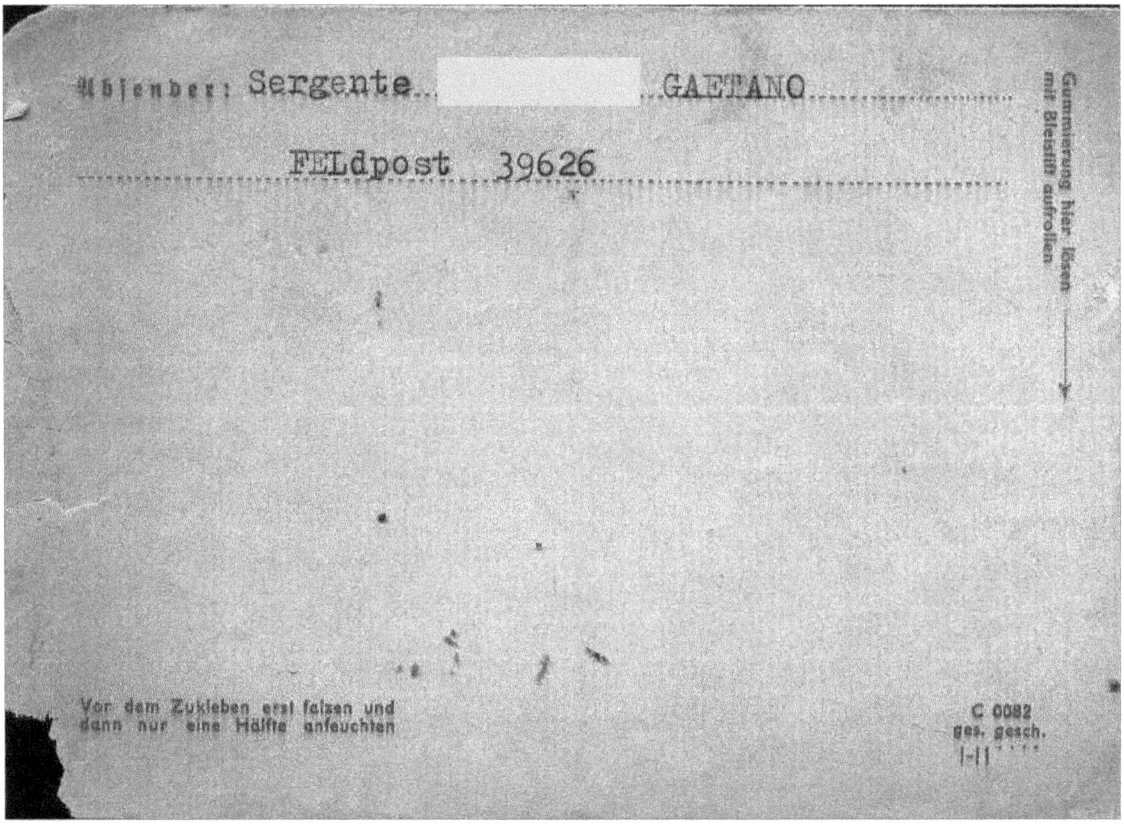

▲ Back of the same envelope as the previous page.

►▼ English source document describing the operation of a fog machine used in Germany (https://miles.forumcommunity.net/?t=62412956&st=15).

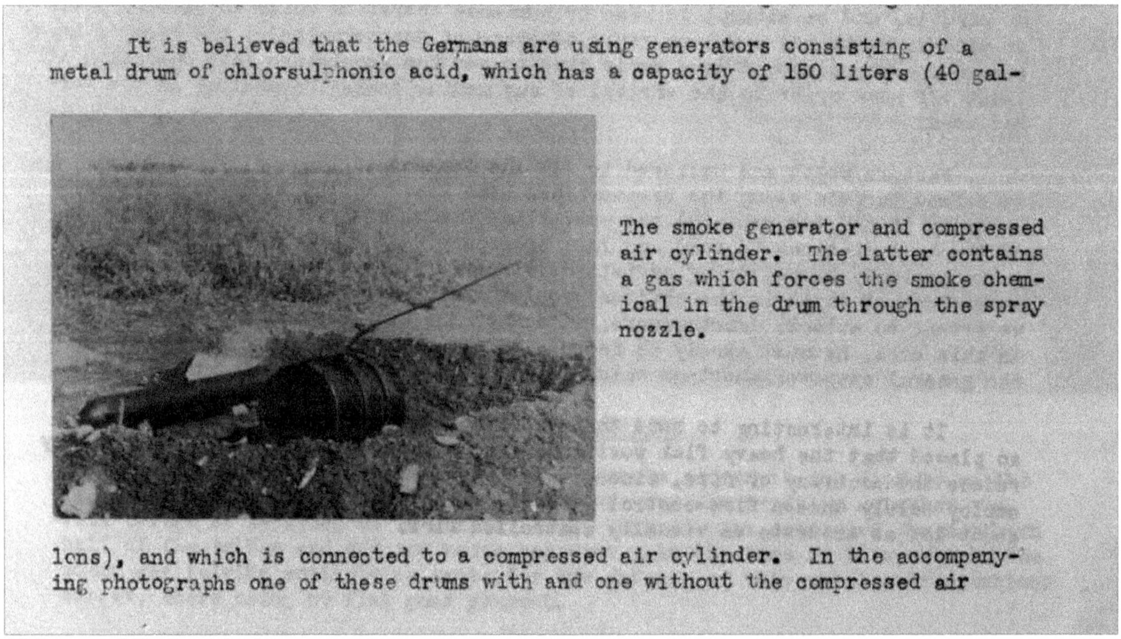

It is believed that the Germans are using generators consisting of a metal drum of chlorsulphonic acid, which has a capacity of 150 liters (40 gal-

The smoke generator and compressed air cylinder. The latter contains a gas which forces the smoke chemical in the drum through the spray nozzle.

lons), and which is connected to a compressed air cylinder. In the accompanying photographs one of these drums with and one without the compressed air cylinder are shown. The acid is expelled through a nozzle at a rate which can be varied as required from 1/2 liter to 2 liters per minute. Each generator is turned on manually, and one or more spare drums of acid are normally kept on

The smoke generator, which has a capacity of 150 liters (40 gallons) of chlorsulphonic acid, showing method of manual control.

hand for quick replacement. Effective densities can be accomplished in about 20 minutes, and an attempt is made to commence operation 30 to 40 minutes prior to attack. With his complete radar coverage of Northern Italy, the enemy's smoke screen operators should have ample time to set the generators into operation at least 1/2 hour prior to the arrival of our medium bomber formations in the target area.

IL „SARACENO"

N. 2 — Anno I.

Periodico Quindicinale dei Nebbiogeni del "I. Btg."

NOTIZIARIO

Dalla R. S. I.

Dall'Italia invasa

Dall'Estero

ULTIME DI CRONACA

Colpo di scena al processo Roatta

VITA e LIBERTA'

"Col concetto di vita, logica conseguenziale è quella di libertà non perchè occorra a noi, per svolgere l'articolo, ma perchè così è nella legge naturale, e nessuno potrà negare l'evidenza dei fatti a meno che non sia la voce dell'America che parli e un italiano anglofilo che ascolti.

Evidentemente il concetto di vita non è nella sua minima espressione come quello di libertà. Per noi l'espressione minima di vita è vivere! L'espressione minima di libertà tutto quello che volete all'infuori della pandemia italiana sull'argomento, post 25 Luglio. Non occorre spremere il cervello per cercare una descrizione efficace: ce la fornisce la "Corrispondenza Repubblicana" del Novembre u. s. in cui ravvisiamo uno stile noto.

"Dinanzi alla tragica babele sgorgata come d'incanto dal colpo di stato del 25 Luglio i rappresentanti della gerontocrazia che l'avevano determinata, cercarono di giustificarla facendosi usbergo di una parola ripetuta in ogni occasione: "libertà". Strana libertà: imposta dall'alto e controllata dalle baionette dell'esercito regio e dal coprifuoco; essa [illegible] per la stampa e vietava la riunione a più di tre persone. E tale libertà costituzionale, che toglieva ogni parvenza di legalità alla legislazione e all'azione statale imponendosi e sovrapponendosi all'esercizio stesso della magistratura, fu regalata agli italiani. Intanto, consce ed inconscie marionette del turpe gioco monarchico, gli uomini dei sette partiti esaltavano sui giornali della penisola quella libertà riconquistata che appariva lampantemente dagli spazi bianchi che la censura imponeva ai loro articoli laudatori. Nel nome, nel regno e nel [illegible] della libertà badogliana, miracoloso elisir, si convincevano alla monarchia capi comunisti e repubblicani.

Questo vento di follia spirò sull'Italia, un'Italia tragicamente provata e già invasa da un nemico, per 45 giorni; e mentre si scalpellavano, in nome della libertà e per ordine del governo i fasci littori dalle facciate dei sanatori, convalescenziari e asili infantili si lasciavano morire uomini e bambini sepolti sotto le macerie provocate dai liberatori.

Nel ricordo di tutto questo, bene sarebbe che gli italiani di ogni partito e di ogni tendenza politica meditassero su i nuovi principi della costituzione Repubblicana, dicessero, in omaggio alla libertà di critica instaurata, le loro idee i loro concetti di libertà di massa, se ce ne può essere uno che superi quello di socializzazione. Resta naturalmente da domandarsi se la coscienza del popolo italiano è passata attraverso una eclissi o si avvia ad un definitivo tramonto.

STAMPA

„Durante l'occupazione dei tedeschi, furono immediatamente bruciati negli archivi del Vaticano, tutti i documenti che potevano compromettere gli ebrei accettati nella città del Vaticano". Il „Popolo" se ne compiace.

Noi vorremmo chiedere a Papa Pacelli: Chi fu a non permettere che la furia bolscevica bruciasse e distruggesse chiese ed immagini sacre, provvedimenti e poteri della chiesa?

Chi fu a dare la possibilità a Papa Pacelli di passeggiare per Roma indisturbato, altezzoso e con seguito, come un vero monarca?

Vorremmo concludere che la cosa ci pare molto semplice: se le masse italiane sono autenticamente rivoluzionarie, capaci cioè di azionare una nuova struttura sociale e quindi capaci di vita e libertà, o sono una mandria incontrollata che attende il padrone.

S. Ten. [illegible]

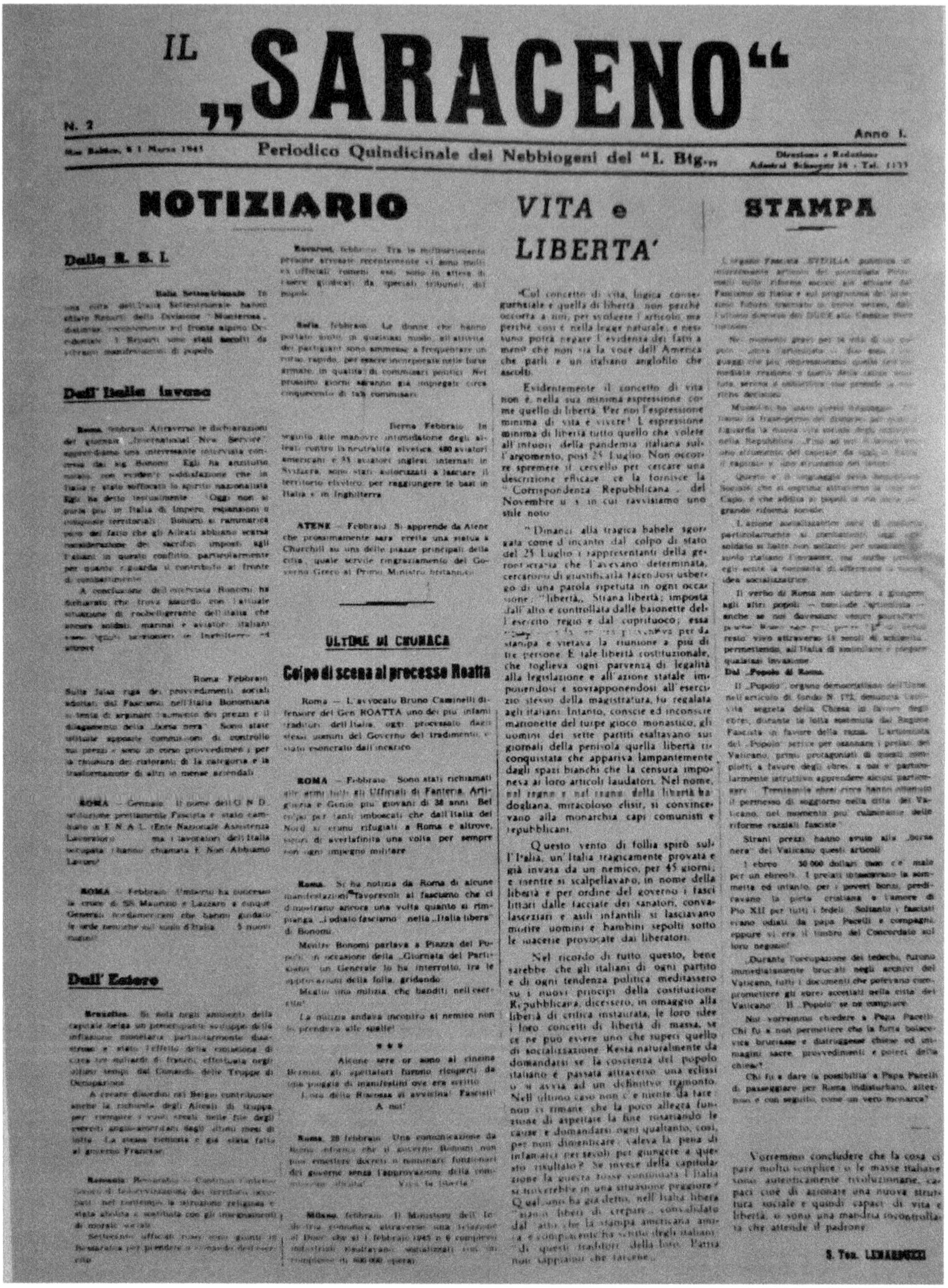

▲ The 1st Fogging Battalion had its own fortnightly printed periodical, called 'Il Saraceno' (The Saracen), in which articles related to civil life in the distant homeland, military events concerning the Armed Forces of the Italian Social Republic, as well as articles with a social slant and political reflections by the officers of the Fogging appeared. This picture shows the front page of issue no. 2 of 1 March 1945 (Pisanò Archive).

LA DOMENICA DEL CORRIERE

Supplemento illustrato del "Corriere della Sera"

Anno 47 — N. 15 — 15 Aprile 1945-XXIII — L. 2,— la copia

Soldati dell'Esercito repubblicano sul fronte del Baltico: durante una violenta azione in una piazzaforte della Prussia orientale, un reparto nebbiogeni del Battaglione "Mussolini", dopo aver assolto il compito della propria specialità, partecipa con le armi in pugno ai furiosi combattimenti che infliggono gravi perdite alle formazioni bolsceviche. (Disegno di B. Albertarelli).

◄ (Previous page) The Fogging Battalions proved to be combative until the last day of the war, so much so that they repeatedly aroused the interest of the R.S.I. press, both the purely military press, such as the Armed Forces magazine 'Gladio', and the civilian press, right up to the last days of the war. In fact, the illustration on the cover of this issue of 'La Domenica del Corriere' of 15 April 1945, created by the illustrator Albertarelli and published only 10 days after the final collapse in Italy, shows some elements of a Fogging Battalion in action during an enemy attack. The caption reads: *'Soldiers of the Republican Army on the Baltic front: during a violent action in a stronghold of East Prussia, a Fogging unit of the "Mussolini" Battalion, after having fulfilled the task of its speciality, participates with weapons in its fist in the furious fighting that inflicts heavy losses on the Bolshevik formations'*. The emphatic tone of the text is typical of the period; it is also unclear why the unit was referred to as the 'Mussolini' Battalion, as it is not clear from the documentation found that any unit used this appellation (private collection).

▼ The text of the Extraordinary Order of the Day number 3 of 24 April 1945, which Captain Raffaele di Pietro, commander of the I Battalion Fogging, sent to his men, which followed the eulogy of Colonel Fedi, reported in the Order of the Day number 49 of 19 April 1945. This extraordinary Order of the Day by Captain Di Pietro also appeared in the magazine "Il Saraceno" (Acta Archive).

> Tale elogio, aggiunto al precedente ed alle due citazioni sull'ordine del giorno del Comando Germanico della Piazzaforte di Swinemünde, rappresenta un privilegio veramente unico del nostro Battaglione tra tutti i reparti nebbiogeni dell'Italia Repubblicana.
>
> La nostra attività, modesta ma preziosa, silenziosa ma non misconosciuta, viene così ancora una volta premiata con il migliore dei premi: il compiacimento dei nostri Comandi che giunge al cuore ed all'animo d'ogni buon soldato come voce della Patria, generosa e riconoscente per chi, ovunque e comunque, sappia dare tutto per essa.
>
> All'encomio del Comando Truppe Nebbiogene aggiungo il mio compiacimento per tutti i miei uomini in genere ed in particolare per i Comandanti di Compagnia ed i Capi Postazione che, fra tutti, costituiscono l'ossatura principale del reparto per il complesso dell'attività da essi richiesta e da essi svolta con intelligenza, volenterosità e disciplina.
>
> Il I. Battaglione mantiene oggi il suo posto di combattimento con lo stesso spirito, con la stessa disciplina, con la stessa prestanza di ieri e di sempre; per me, personalmente, è particolare privilegio e fonte d'alte soddisfazioni esserne il Comandante.
>
> Miei soldati: voi avete compiuto onestamente e disciplinatamente il vostro dovere di fronte alla Patria, alla famiglia, ed alla nostra coscienza. Comunque volgano le sorti della guerra voi tornerete in Patria con la fronte alta, con lo spirito sereno degli uomini onesti e con il nome d'Italia profondamente racchiuso nel vostro cuore.
>
> Con uomini come voi l'Italia non potrà non essere libera, grande, imperiale come il Destino l'aveva designata e come essa è realmente stata fino alle fatidiche, ed infami date del 25 Luglio ed 8 Settembre 1943.-
>
> Viva l'Italia!
>
> IL CAPITANO
> COMANDANTE DEL BATTAGLIONE
> (Di Pietro Raffaele)

BIBLIOGRAPHY

BOOKS

- AA.VV., "Repubblica Sociale Italiana - Storia", Centro Editoriale Nazionale, Roma, 1959.
- AA.VV., "Soldati e Battaglie della Seconda Guerra Mondiale", Hobby & Work Italiana Editrice, Bresso (MI), 1999.
- Arena Nino, "Italia in guerra 1040/45", Ermanno Albertelli Editore, Parma, 1997.
- Arena Nino, "R.S.I. – Forze Armate della Repubblica Sociale – La guerra in Italia – 1943 – 1944 – 1945", Ermanno Albertelli Editore, Parma, 2002.
- Bobbio Roberto, Cucut Carlo, "Attilio Viziano – Ricordi di un corrispondente di guerra", Marvia Edizioni, Voghera (PV), 2008.
- Cucut Carlo, "Le Forze Armate della R.S.I. – Forze di terra", GMT, Trento, 2005.
- Greve Friedrich August, "Die Luftverteidigung im Abschnitt Wilhelmshaven 1939-1945", Hermann Lüers, Jever (Germania), 1999.
- Jowett Philip, "The Italian Army 1940 – 45 (3)", serie "Men-at-Arms", Osprey Military, UK, 2001.
- Kuchler Heinz, "Fregi, mostrine, distintivi della R.S.I.", Intergest, Milano, 1976.
- Marzetti Paolo, " Uniformi e distintivi italiani 1933 – 1945", Ermanno Albertelli Editore, Parma 1995.
- Montagnani Marco, Zarcone Antonino, Cappellano Filippo, "Il Servizio Chimico militare 1923 – 1945 – Storia, ordinamento, equipaggiamenti", Ufficio Storico dello Stato Maggiore dell'Esercito, Roma, 2011.
- Morera Renzo, "Dentro la Missione Militare in Germania della R.S.I. - Storia di un soldato dell'ultimo Mussolini", S.I.P., Roma, 2010.
- Pisanò Giorgio, "Storia della Guerra Civile in Italia", Edizioni F.P.E., Milano, 1967.
- Pisanò Giorgio, "Gli ultimi in grigioverde", Edizioni F.P.E., Milano, 1994.
- Rocco Giuseppe, "Con l'Onore per l'Onore – L'organizzazione militare della R.S.I." Greco & Greco, Milano, 1998.
- Rosignoli Guido, "RSI – Uniformi, distintivi, equipaggiamenti ed armi 1943 – 1945", Ermanno Albertelli Editore, Parma, 1998.
- Sparacino Fausto, "Distintivi e medaglie della R.S.I.", E.M.I. – serie "Militaria", Milano, 1988.
- Sparacino Fausto, "Distintivi e medaglie della R.S.I., della Legione SS Italiana e dei Veterani della R.S.I", E.M.I. – serie "Militaria", Milano, 1994.

ARTICLES

- "A fronte alta anche sul Baltico per la Patria e l'idea socializzatrice" in ACTA n°11 (marzo – maggio 1990), Istituto Storico ella RSI.
- "Battaglioni Nebbiogeni della R.S.I. fino al 3 maggio 1945 in Nord Europa" in ACTA n° 21 (maggio/luglio 1993), Istituto Storico della RSI.
- "La Missione Militare in Germania del Ministero delle Forze Armate della R.S.I." in ACTA n°25 (settembre-novembre 1994), Istituto Storico ella RSI.
- "A Stettino il III Battaglione Nebbiogeno della RSI istruì la Kriegsmarine" in ACTA n° 55 (settembre/novembre 2004), Istituto Storico della RSI.
- "Combattente per la libertà, propria" in ACTA n° 72 (maggio/luglio 2010), Istituto Storico della RSI.
- Crippa Paolo, "Italian "Nebbiogeni" Battalions on the Baltic Sea" in "The Axis Forces" n° 12, dicembre 2019.
- Cucut Carlo, "I REPARTI NEBBIOGENI ITALIANI IN GERMANIA, 1942-1945" in "Storia Militare" n° 353, febbraio 2023
- Cucut Carlo, "I Reparti nebbiogeni italiani in Germania. Storia dei militari italiani del Genio sul Baltico" in SGM Seconda Guerra Mondiale n° 2, ottobre 2008

Other publications

- Conti Arturo, "Albo dei Caduti e dei Dispersi della Repubblica Sociale Italiana", Fondazione della R.S.I. – Istituto Storico, Terranuova Bracciolini (AR), 2019.
- "Elenco "Livio Valentini" - Caduti Repubblica Sociale Italiana", 2020.

Other documents

- Lettera del capitano Raffaele Di Pietro a Pieramedeo Baldrati del 12 settembre 1967 (copia fotostatica in possesso dell'autore).
- Documenti della serie T-1022 della N.A.R.A.- National Archives and Records Administration.

TITOLI GIÀ PUBBLICATI - TITLES ALREADY PUBLISHING

BOOKS TO COLLECT

www.ingramcontent.com/pod-product-compliance
Lightning Source LLC
LaVergne TN
LVHW072119060526
838201LV00068B/4925